PAULETTE RAMSAY gr
Jamaica. She studied at the
she obtained her Ph.D degr
at the University of Florida,
Venezuela, Spain and the Do   ...l published
articles, translations, reviews   ...views have appeared in
several academic journals. She has been an Assistant Professor
in the Foreign Languages Department at Berry College in the
USA and is currently a Lecturer in the Department of
Language, Linguistics and Philosophy at the University of the
West Indies, Mona campus, in Kingston, Jamaica. She has a
special interest in the literary production and culture of Afro-
Hispanic societies.

PAULETTE RAMSAY

AUNT JEN

Orders: please contact Bookpoint Ltd, 130 Park Drive, Milton Park, Abingdon, Oxon
OX14 4SE. Telephone: (44) 01235 827720. Fax: (44) 01235 400454. Email education@
bookpoint.co.uk. Lines are open from 9 a.m. to 5 p.m., Monday to Saturday, with a
24-hour message answering service. You can also order through our website:
www.hoddereducation.com

First published by Heinemann Educational Publishers in 2002
Published from 2015 by Hodder Education,
An Hachette UK Company
Carmelite House
50 Victoria Embankment
London EC4Y 0DZ
www.hoddereducation.com

British Library Cataloguing in Publication Data
A catalogue record for this book is available from the British Library.

Phototypeset by SetSystems Ltd, Saffron Walden, Essex

Author photograph by M. Smith

Printed and bound by CPI Group (UK) Ltd, Croydon, CR0 4YY

ISBN 978 0 4359 1012 9

ARP Impression 101

Dear Aunt Jen,

Last night I had a very bad dream. I dreamt that I was on a ship which was sinking. I jumped from the ship to try to swim to shore but I began to sink. You were also on the ship and you jumped off to try and rescue me but as I reached out to grab your hand you turned into a River Mumma and swam away.

I told Ma about my dream and she said is not a good one. She said that a River Mumma is a sign of bad luck and she doesn't like it at all at all. She asked me to describe the ship and when I did, she said that it looked just like the one you went to England on.

This is the third time I'm dreaming about you. The first time, I dreamt that you were standing in a boat in John's River and you were calling me but when I started to come towards you you disappeared and left the empty boat rocking from side to side.

In the second dream I saw you boarding a boat with some other people. I decided to follow you on to the boat and I was just about to put my foot on the plank when a big, tall, strapping man pulled it up and the boat sailed away.

You didn't have a face in the dreams. Well, maybe I just didn't see your face, but I know it was you. In any case, I don't know what your face looks like – I really don't remember. But I know that you are the woman I saw in my three dreams. Something, I can't explain what, makes me know it was you.

That is why I decided to write to you. I asked Ma if she thought it was a good idea to write to you and she said she will neither say yeah nor nay. She said maybe if she was me she wouldn't write but she not me so I must decide for myself cause is ebry dankey to him sankey. So I decided to write.

Apart from telling you about my dreams I don't really have much to say. In any case Ma says when you are writing someone for the first time the letter should not be too long.

The part I find strange about my second dream is that you didn't seem to see me at all. You walked away with the other people without seeming to notice that I was there. Anyway, I want to ask you before I close if you ever dream about me and can you send a picture of yourself for me?

Ma says I must never ask anyone for anything, but it's just a picture, so maybe that is not so bad.

Bye,

Sunshine

27 May 1970

Dear Aunt Jen,

It's been three months since I wrote to you and I have been going to the post office every day to see if you replied to my letter. Ma said give it one month for my letter to get to you and another month for your reply to get to Jamaica but still I haven't got a letter from you.

I am thinking that maybe you didn't reply because you are upset that I called you Aunt Jen in my letter. Maybe you think that is too familiar. Ma always says familiarity breeds contempt. I mentioned it to Ma but she said not at all because is jus a name and you couldn't be so finniki about a name. I did not explain in my first letter that everybody in the house here always calls you Aunt Jen. Ma always says to me, 'You Aunt Jen sen some money for you or you Aunt Jen say she sendin a parcel for you.' I always call you Aunt Jen in my mind.

So I hope that is not why you did not reply. Well if that was why you can reply to me now that I explained it all. I am anxious to get your letter.

Love,

Sunshine

PS: Please remember the photograph.

3 June 1970

Dear Aunt Jen,

I got a letter from Uncle Roy today. He writes to me very often. He says he always thinks of me as his daughter because I used to call him 'Dada' when I was little. It's funny but I think of him as my father too. I remember how he used to play with me and tickle me. He would throw me up in the air, catch me and put me down and then run and hide and shout, 'Come an fine me!' I used to have so much fun searching for him under the beds, behind the doors and in the closets. One day he hid in Gramps' big hamper basket and I couldn't find him until Ma showed me where he was. Ma used to say he was just like a lickle chile, so jokify, but he was just happy and loved to make me happy too. I remember everything just like it was yesterday.

I cried so much when he went to America, but I was very happy when I got his first letter and now even though I still miss him a lot, I love to get his letters. He sent me a picture of himself with his wife. She looks like a nice lady. Her face is sort of pretty, not very pretty, but she looks all right. I was wondering if you would look like her in your picture, or maybe better.

3

I told Uncle Roy that I wrote to you and you have not replied. He said he would talk to you about it. I didn't tell him to ask you anything. I just told him that you never reply to any of my letters. Anyway, I hope he gets you to write to me. He says he doesn't think you are vexed with me about anything, but maybe you're just working hard right now.

Ma is a bit upset with you for not replying to my letters. She does not say so to me though and I know she doesn't want me to know that she is upset because when I ask her why she thinks you did not reply she says I must jus be patient. But the way her face changes every time I ask her about it makes me realise that she is not pleased.

Anyway, I was just sitting down doing nothing so I thought I would write to you. Actually, I like to write. Sometimes I write poems or letters to myself so I enjoy doing it. Sometimes I think that maybe you didn't get my letters. Sometimes letters get lost. Still it would be strange if my two letters to you got lost. Uncle Roy always gets my letters.

I am going to end the letter now because I hear Ma calling me. I think she wants me to go to the shop to buy something. Every time I go to the shop Miss Mabel asks me, 'Sunshine, how is your Aunt Jen?' I always say, 'Fine ma'am.' That's what Ma tells everybody when they ask her, except Aunt Sue. Sometimes I hear her telling Aunt Sue that she hasn't got a letter from you for a long time and sometimes she tells her that you sent an empty letter even though she told you things hard hard. Anyway, she says she prays for you night and day because she doesn't know if your life in England is rough or easy. You don't tell her the full full story, she told Aunt Sue. Anyway, the last time I went to the shop, Miss Mabel said to tell you that it's time for you to come back to Jamaica and look at your old friends' faces before they die. She asked me if you didn't have any plans to come back to Jamaica this year and I told her that

I didn't think so. When I told Ma she said Miss Mabel is a nice lady, but she mind everybody business. Ma says I must realise that people will always ask questions but shet mouth don't ketch fly.

Well, this is a very long letter so I will end it now. I hope you get it and reply to me soon. I am looking forward to your letter and photograph.

Love,
Sunshine

PS: This morning when I told Ma I wrote you another letter she just looked at me and said, 'Sunshine, less turkey, less yaws.'

26 June 1970

Dear Aunt Jen,

I sat and thought about you for a long time today. I tried to picture you in England, walking, talking, going to work. I keep wondering what you are doing and thinking about. I think you must be a busy busy lady why you haven't replied to my letter. I thought you would be so happy to get a letter from me that you would write to me quick quick.

I'm trying to remember what you looked like when you were here but the only thing I remember is when you used to take all of us children to buy ice cream at Miss Mabel's shop on Sunday evenings. I was the littlest one and sometimes Pam would say, 'Aunt Jen Sunshine wastin her ice cream' and you would say, 'Is awright Pam she is jus enjoyin it.' I don't remember what you look like though. Why don't you send a picture?

I told Ma what I remember the other day, but she said she doesn't think I remember anything about you at all because I was so young when you and Pam were here. She says I'm mixing it up with something else that happened with somebody else. Ma says that Pam's mother came for her right after you left and Willie's mother came for him exactly one year after that and I was only about three at that time so there is no way that I could remember these things. But I know what I remember.

I can't write you a longer letter because I hear Ma calling me. She says I spend too much time writing writing and my writing getting me nowhere. She's not in a good mood today because she can't find her teeth. She took them out and she can't remember where she put them, so she's really miserable. I have to stop now.

Sunshine

PS: I just had a funny feeling that maybe you're not getting my letters. I am sure you would not get my letters and not reply to me.

5 July 1970

Dear Aunt Jen,

Ma thinks I should stop pushing up on you. She says if you want to write you will write and I must stop badda badda you. Last night I heard her telling Aunt Sue that she cannot believe that a daughter of hers would treat her own child the way you are treating me. She didn't know I was listening but she told Aunt Sue that she's not going to let me write any more letters to you until you reply. She doesn't know that I'm writing this one or she would be very upset with me.

Last night I opened the box that Ma keeps your old things in. I searched and searched for a photograph but I didn't find any. I only found some figurines, your old clothes, some books and your letters to God. Oh, I almost forgot the wigs! I was really surprised to see all those wigs. I cannot imagine why you would need to wear all those different wigs. I think they are all ugly and the hair looks like goat's hair. I would never wear those things on my head. I prefer my own hair. I think it's softer and prettier than those wigs. Anyway, I hid and read the letters. There was one very short one which is still puzzling my mind because all it said was:

Dear God,
    Je veux quitter cet endroit.

I can't tell Ma about it because she always says I am not to interfere with that box. I didn't even know that you knew another language. I had to doublecheck the letter to make sure I'm spelling the words correctly here. You can send and tell me what it means.

Anxious to hear from you,
Sunshine

PS: Sometimes I wish I could see you face to face to talk to you.

7

19 July 1970

Dear Aunt Jen,

I can't wait to get your letter before I write to you. I feel that what I have to tell you is so important that I must write and tell you right away.

Ma went to Madda Penny about my dreams yesterday. She said Madda Penny said they are serious serious dreams and she doesn't like what she's seeing at all. She told Ma that she could only tell her the meaning of the second dream because she needed me before her, so she could read me up and see what the first and third dreams mean.

She says the second dream means that you have a man who plays an important part in your life. She says he is a strong man. He is domineering. He rules you. He controls you. She says you are afraid of him and he doesn't know that you have a child in Jamaica. She says the dream means that when he finds out about me he is going to cut off all communication between us, just like how the man in the dream pulled up the plank and prevented me from getting to you.

Ma says she'll take me to hear what the other two dreams mean next week when Uncle Johnny gets paid and gives her some money. She says I'm to wait until I know the meaning of the other two dreams before I write and tell you anything. But I can't wait for two weeks before asking you if any part of Madda Penny's interpretation of the dream is true. Do you really have a man who is ruling your life? Did you get married again?

I really don't think you have, because you would tell Ma and Uncle Roy, and Uncle Roy would tell me. In any case I heard Ma tell Aunt Sue that your life is mashed up for ever because my father says he's not giving you the divorce and you won't be able to marry another man. So I'm thinking that maybe Madda Penny is not so good at interpreting dreams because her explanation makes it seem as if you are married again and Ma said she was sure you can't marry again. I have to go now, Ma is calling me.

(Two days later)

I am just getting a chance to finish this letter. Ma caught me writing it and said that this writing writing thing is going to damage my eyes. She says I do too much reading already and if I add all this writing writing to it my eyes will go right back to where she brought them from. Every time Ma thinks that I'm using my eyes too much, as she puts it, she talks about where she brought them from. Even though I know that nothing will happen to my eyes, every time she says that she makes me a little worried. I wouldn't want my eyes to go back to where Ma took them from. That was a long time ago – about seven years to be exact. I woke up one morning and my two eyes were red like ackee pods, as Ma put it. They itched and itched and itched. Nobody could figure out what happened to them. Ma took me to Lucea every Friday to an eye specialist but he said he didn't know what to do to stop the itching and clear up the redness. Even now when I think about it I can feel the itching. Ma gave me carrot juice every day until I hated the sight of carrots. That didn't help. Every week somebody else came to Ma with a different remedy. None of them worked.

One day Granny P. came and told Ma that she heard about a remedy that would cure my eyes. Ma decided to try it. She would try anything at that stage. So every morning she woke me up early early to wash my face in the dew on Gramps' dasheen and coco leaves. That was bad enough but after that I had to go to Blossom's house (Aunty Mirrie's daughter) and she would squeeze milk from her breasts into my eyes. Well, I don't know if it was the milk or the dew or both that worked but my eyes got better quick quick after that. The itching stopped and the redness cleared up. Every time I look at Blossom's son now I remember how I used to get some of his milk in my eyes.

I really wouldn't want my eyes to go back to where Ma brought them from, but I don't think that writing these two little letters will do anything to them. I will just make sure that Ma doesn't see me writing. I have to go now, but I hope to get a letter from you soon.

Until I hear from you,

Sunshine

PS: There is so much you don't know about me and there are so many questions that I have for you. I'm sure you will explain everything when you write and I know that your letter will be very long because you have a lot of things to tell me. Please write soon and don't forget the photograph. Send one which shows your face plain plain.

30 July 1970

Dear Aunt Jen,

I hope you're feeling better now. Uncle Roy wrote to me and told me that he phoned you and you told him that you were very, very sick, almost at death's door, that is why you didn't reply to any of my letters.

I am so ashamed of myself that I was putting so much pressure on you to write to me. I should know that something was wrong with you why you didn't write. I hope you will understand that I just got anxious because I wanted my own letter from you. I really hope you are feeling better and that you'll soon be able to get back to work.

Ma didn't take me to Madda Penny last week because she said that Uncle Johnny gave her less than the usual amount of money and she couldn't afford to pay Madda Penny out of that. She can't ask Gramps for the money because he says Madda Penny is a big jinnal and Ma is just wasting money every time she goes to her, so she says I'll have to wait until Uncle Roy sends some money.

I think that Ma has changed her mind about you since she heard that you are sick. Aunt Sue told her that she should know that something was wrong with you, why you didn't answer your own child or send money for her for over four months. Well to tell the truth that was the first time I was hearing that you haven't sent money to Ma for me. Ma would never tell me that. Anyway she agreed with Aunt Sue and she's going to write to you tonight. She was singing her favourite song all of this evening – 'Sweet Jesus, Sweet Jesus, what a wonda you are . . .'. She was singing it in the low, sweet nightingale voice she uses when she's happy. Whenever she sings like that, a nice warm feeling comes over the house just as if she's singing a lullaby and putting everybody to sleep. I haven't heard her sing it for a long time, so I know she's happy. She's happy to hear about you.

Well, take care of yourself and write to me when you can. There's no rush.

Love,

~~Your d~~

Sunshine

PS: Ma says I'm not to worry, you'll soon write because chip don't fall far from block.

Dear Aunt Jen,

Time flies so fast! Yesterday I looked at the calendar and realised that tomorrow will make seven months since I wrote the first letter to you.

Well, I'm not really complaining about not getting any reply from you as yet, because I know you are still recovering from your illness. As soon as you feel better you must write to me because I am really worrying about you. I know that Ma is also anxious to know if you are better. She prays for you all the time and I heard her telling Aunt Sue that you are not as tough as she is and maybe you should come home. She also told Aunt Sue not to let anyone in the district know that you not doing well, she must just help her to pray for you. I know that Aunt Sue will not tell anyone. Ma tells her all her problems and secrets and she tells Ma hers and the two of them always say that what they hear from each other will never pass their lips. Ma says Aunt Sue is nicer now that her husband is dead. She says he was too cobitch. Sometimes Ma says some things I have to wonder if she really means them.

Ma always says that Aunt Sue is like a rock because she can always depend on her to encourage her when she's feeling low. Gramps says that Ma talks to Aunt Sue more than she talks to him but Ma says that's because he is not interested in anything but his animals, his land and his pipe. Well, I don't know if Ma talks to Aunt Sue more but I know that Aunt Sue listens when Ma is talking to her and she encourages Ma to be cheerful and not to worry. When Ma talks to Gramps he just grunts or shakes his head and that upsets Ma. So she prefers to talk to Aunt Sue. I like her too, even though she's so wiry. She lickle but she tallawah as Ma would say. She is strong and sure of herself and she always has the right words to set people's mind at ease. Most of all I love her baking. She makes nicer duckunoos and gizadas than Ma and she always makes some for me when she bakes. I love when she comes on Fridays, because I can always count on her to bring some of the nice totoes or grater cakes or gizadas which she makes on Thursdays. She says I enjoy her baking just like you used to.

Yesterday she went to Madda Penny to ask her about her own private business. I am sure she told Ma but I don't know what it is. Anyway, she said that Madda Penny told her to tell her friend, that is Ma, that she needs to come to her so she can tell her the meaning of the other two dreams. Ma says that means that the two dreams really mean something bad is going to happen, so she's going to try her best to find the money to go before the week runs out.

I think that now that Ma knows that you were sick, she thinks that the dreams have something to do with your sickness. I don't know what to think, so I'll just wait to hear what Madda Penny says. I hope that Ma will have the money to go tomorrow.

I think I have a little idea of what you look like now. At least I think so because of something that Uncle Eddy said the other day when he came to visit Ma. I was combing my hair in front of the mirror and he said, 'Sunshine, you vain jus like you madda. An you is the dead stamp of har. They could cut off you head and put on har own and nobody could tell the difference. Ah wonder what she look like now. She was a beautiful black girl.' Since then, every now and then I stand in front of the mirror and stare at my face and pretend that I'm looking at you. I am wondering if Uncle Eddy means that I'm a pretty black girl too, but I don't have the courage to ask him.

I still need your photograph though, that is what will really tell me what you look like – that is until I see you face to face. I am looking forward to that day.

Love,
Sunshine

25 September 1970

Dear Aunt Jen,

I got tired of teaching the hibiscus hedge six and seven times and I'm not in the mood to study right now, so I decided to write to you. I think this letter writing thing is fast becoming my hobby.

I went to see Granny P. this morning. I visit her every other Saturday. I like to visit her. She makes me feel nice and warm when she puts her arms around me and pulls me against her bosom. When I was little she would squeeze me until I felt like I was stifling, then she would push me away from her and say, 'We have to comb this hair. Whoever comb it don't know that they should take the hair out of you pretty face, eeh?' And she would put me to sit under the breadfruit tree, take her comb out of her apron pocket, pull out my hair and comb it all over. When she was finished, she would step back and look at me and say, 'That is how I like to see you face.'

She told me this morning that she's proud of the nice young lady I'm growing up to be. She says I must always walk the straight and narrow path, keep myself circumspec and stay away from bad company because if you sleep with dog you ketch dem flea. As usual when I was leaving she reminded me that I always have a place to stay at her house. She said that if anything ever happens to Ma or Gramps she will be happy for me to live with her. She says she knows you wouldn't mind. I would willingly live with her because even though she's a no-nononsense person, she is kind. I'm sure I would get along with her – she doesn't quarrel and shout when she's speaking her mind, she simply tells you what she's thinking. That is a peaceful way to live.

Speaking of living peacefully, Uncle Johnny came home stone drunk last night and created such a rumpus he woke up the whole district. He was like a volcano which erupted without any warning. He bellowed out some bad words long from here to Cross Roads and back. I still can't believe that was Uncle Johnny. He cursed Mr Dennis who he says is a wicked slave driver because he doesn't pay him a proper salary for all the work he does for him. He cursed Mrs Chung, who he says over-prices her goods so he has to pay her half his salary when he wants to buy a decent shirt to put on his back. He cursed the tractor which he drives for Mr Dennis because he says it's slower than Mr Walcott's old mule. He cursed the long-face cow he bought from Moses Johnson because he thought it would have about two calves by now, so he could sell them and make a profit. He cursed you for not writing to me so that every night I have all kinds of fool-fool dreams about you to make Ma want his money to go to Madda Penny for interpretation. When Gramps told him to stop disturbing the peace in the house, he said nobody would be at peace until he leaves Mr Dennis' half-dead job and goes to America to earn good money. Gramps told him that he will give him the money for his plane fare when he sells the next crop of rice.

I've never seen Uncle Johnny behave like that. He must have been very frustrated because he is always so easy-going and jovial that nobody would suspect that he has a problem. I felt so sorry for him when he threw himself on his bed and bawled like a baby after Gramps said he would help him to go

15

to America. He screamed like when Ma's kettle is letting out steam. We all stood at the door listening and watching helplessly until he became quiet. Gramps threw a sheet over him and left him to sleep. Poor Uncle Johnny. I don't want him to go, because I won't have anyone to play dominoes and cards with me. Sometimes when I try to cheat in a game he tickles me until I feel like I'm going to faint. When I say, 'No, Mister Johnny Scarlet, I won't cheat again,' he stops tickling me and says, 'A cheatin woman is an abomination to the Lord.' I want Uncle Johnny to find a better job and be happy but I don't want him to go. It will be just like when Uncle Roy left. It seems that all my favourite people always leave. I don't like America and England. Everybody I want around me goes away to these places. I will never go to England or America when I'm big, I'm staying right here.

When we left the room, I asked Gramps if he would really help Uncle Johnny to go to America, and after a long silence he said, yes, as much as it pains his heart to see his last child go, he will help if it will make him happy. He said he would never in a million years guess that Johnny has so much pain bottled up inside of him. Gramps sounded like it pained him to talk about it. Ma has not said a word about it. She never likes any of us to talk too loudly in the house. She is always quick to tell us that bush have ears. But last night she couldn't even find those words. I think she was shocked. She always says that Uncle Johnny is such a decent young man. I have a funny suspicion that that is why she left so early this morning to go to Aunt Sue's house. I think they are going to pray and fast for Uncle Johnny all day.

When I peeped into Uncle Johnny's bedroom this morning he was still fast asleep. I think he's totally worn out after all that ranting and raving last night. I can't believe that he had so much worrying about and he didn't let any of us know how he was feeling. In fact he's still sleeping now, unless he's awake but is too ashamed to come out and face Gramps.

Well, all this riot that Uncle Johnny created last night made me get a lot of information from Gramps that maybe I wouldn't get otherwise. It seems as if he was so shaken up by Uncle Johnny's outburst that he couldn't sleep. He sat in his rocking chair smoking his pipe and staring into space for a long time. I went and sat beside him and stared into space too. After a long time I decided to talk to him. I asked him what he was thinking about and he said, in a quiet voice which I would never associate with Gramps, that he was thinking about his children. He told me that he was sad sad when you went away. You were a bright bright girl, doing well in school, but you got mixed up with my father and got into trouble, so he sent you away to Kingston to live with your Aunt Joyce until I was born. He arranged everything so that two years later you were on a ship to England. I told him I thought you were married to my father when I was born, but he said my father didn't stop asking questions until he found out where you were and followed you all the way to England and married you.

The part of this history lesson that surprised me was when Gramps said he was so happy when you came to your senses and left the ugly brute. Gramps said when you decided you wanted to go back to school because you wanted to be a nurse, my father told you that he didn't want his wife to work. Gramps says you quietly packed your things one day when he (my father) was at work and left. Gramps says thank God for that brave brave step, you are a fully qualified nurse today. He says he misses you though, and Uncle Roy, but he doesn't worry about Uncle Roy so much because he can take care of himself. It's you he's concerned about, especially now that you won't reply to my letters and Uncle Roy says you were sick. I couldn't understand why Gramps was so upset that you're away when he was the one who sent you away in the first place. So I asked him why he sent you away if he knew he would miss you so much and he said he sent you to seek you fortune. Well, when I think about this fortune-seeking thing, I think of the people in the storybooks who are always leaving to go and seek their fortune. Most of the time they end up doing something good for a prince or a king or a queen who then takes them to their castle or palace and gives them some of their gold and diamonds and jewels. Sometimes they let them live in the palace or castle with them and dress them up in pretty clothes. The prodigal son in the Bible went to seek his fortune too, only that he didn't have as much luck as the ones in the storybooks and he ended up going back home poor poor poor. I hope you found your fortune by now.

Speaking of palaces and castles, have you been to Buckingham Palace? Have you ever seen the Queen? What does she look like? Every time I think of her, I picture her like one of the big dollies in Miss Matarr's shop in Green Island – just smiling and sitting still to make sure her crown doesn't fall off. Last week in Girl Guides meeting I almost got into trouble with the leader because I asked her which queen we were promising to serve and she said there's only one queen and that is the Queen of England who lives in Buckingham Palace. I told her that I thought there were queens in other parts of the world such as Africa but she said I should not show my ignorance, I must just say the promise and stop asking foolish questions and if I know how many Brownies, Girl Guides, Cub Scouts and Scouts in Jamaica say it every day without asking stupid questions.

Guess what? Gramps just told me that he's going to give Ma the money to go to Madda Penny to see if she can really really figure out these strange dreams that I've had. I was so shocked when he said it, I almost dropped off the chair. Boy, he must really be worried about you! I'm sure Ma will be even more shocked when he gives her the money to go. Can you imagine, Gramps who always says such terrible things about Madda Penny, giving Ma money to go to her? I'm telling you Aunt Jen, now I know that Gramps really loves you. He loves all his children whole heap whole heap. He doesn't talk much but he carries a lot of love deep deep inside of him. I think I started to love him last night too. He changed from being a stony old shadow to being a real Gramps. I wish I could begin to know you too, just like I got to know Gramps a little better last night. I'm keeping my fingers crossed that soon you will be writing to me and telling me a lot about yourself.

Anyway, I have to stop now. This must be the longest letter I've ever written. Take care of yourself.

Love,
Sunshine

PS: As soon as Ma gets the money from Gramps to go to Madda Penny, we will go to her and I will write and tell you what she says about the dreams.

26 September 1970

Dear Aunt Jen,

When I went to mail your letter today I got your card. It is very pretty. Ma was not pleased about it. She said that that is white people style you pick up. So instead of writing a decent letter you jus sen a card saying 'Thinking of you'. She said I should sen it back because we not interested in you thoughts.

I must be honest and tell you though that I was very disappointed too that you didn't include a letter. I would have preferred a letter, even the five-pound note that you included does not mean as much to me as a letter would mean. All you scribbled in the card was 'Your loving mother', not even a 'To Sunshine' or one line to ask me how I am. I read the card over and over and the words sound very wonderful but I'm not so sure they mean very much to me because they really were written by somebody I don't know about in some place I don't know where. To tell you the truth after I thought about it I got so upset that I threw the card through the window. Uncle Johnny took it up and said that since no one ever sends him any cards he'll keep it. He put it to stand on his chest of drawers. When I pass by his bedroom door I close my eyes. I don't like to see the card standing there because it seems as if it's making fun of me – just standing there all the time.

I don't want to sound selfish, but the more I think about it the more I think that after I wrote you several letters, nine to be exact, you could have written me a letter – even six lines – and the least you could do was to send me one of your photographs. I think you are a hard person.

Sunshine

PS: Today Aunt Sue told me that sometimes we have to ben we mind to we condition. She says I must put my head to my books and stop concentrating on all kinds of outside things.

26 September 1970

Dear Aunt Jen,

When I went to mail your letter today I got your card. It is very pretty. Ma was not pleased about it. She said that that is white people style you pick up. So instead of writing a decent letter you just send a card saying 'Thinking of you'. She said I should send it back because we not interested in you thoughts.

I must be honest and tell you though that I was very disappointed too that you didn't include a letter. I don't want to sound selfish, but the more I think about it the more I think that after I wrote you several letters, nine to be exact, you could have written me a letter – even six lines – and the least you could do was to send me one of your photographs.

Sunshine

PS: Ma says to take care of yourself.

26 September 1970

Dear Aunt Jen,
     You have finally replied to my letters. I am so happy. Thank you for the beautiful card which you sent. It is really very pretty. Thank you for the money.

Sunshine

26 September 1970

Dear Aunt Jen,
     I am glad that you have finally replied to my letters. Now I know that they are not lost. I know that your letter was very short because you are still not feeling well. I know that as soon as you are fully recovered you will write Ma a nice long letter.
     Thank you for the money also.
                    Yours respectfully,
                              Sunshine

26 September 1970

Dear Aunt Jen,

It was nice to hear from you at last. I have never seen such a beautiful card before. It's nice. Thank you for the card and for the money.

Sunshine

15 October 1970

Dear Aunt Jen,

I'm writing to tell you that Ma and I went to Madda Penny this morning. Ma didn't take Gramps' money. She says she and Aunt Sue were baking totoes and selling them secretly so she will use her own money to go to Madda. I'm writing because we are all frightened by what Madda Penny said. When Ma came home and told Gramps, he went to bed immediately. Aunt Sue came over and said she thinks the whole family should fast and pray tomorrow to break the hold of this hand that has come upon the family. She says Madda Penny is a genuine Madda Woman, a real visioner, and we all have to take whatever she says serious serious.

Sunshine

Dear Aunt Jen,

I'm writing to tell you that Ma and I went to Madda Penny this morning. Ma didn't take Gramps' money. She says she and Aunt Sue were baking totoes and selling them secretly so she will use her own money to go to Madda. I'm writing because we are all frightened by what Madda Penny said. When Ma came home and told Gramps, he went to bed immediately. Aunt Sue came over and said she thinks the whole family should fast and pray tomorrow to break the hold of this hand that has come upon the family. She says Madda Penny is a genuine Madda Woman, a real visioner, and we all have to take whatever she says serious serious.

I have decided to give you full details of what happened when Ma and I went to Madda Penny. Remember that Madda Penny said that she needed me before her so she could tell the meaning of the other two dreams, so I went with Ma. Ma took me with her when it was her turn to go on the stand. When we stood before her, Madda Penny looked at me and said, 'Child, you waited too long to come to me.' Then she looked at Ma and said, 'Madda, ban you belly! Madda, ban you belly! Sudden death and destruction! Sudden death and destruction.' I looked at Ma's face and she looked as if she was going to faint. Madda Penny started to rock back and forth and roll over her eyes and chant, 'Sudden death! Sudden death!' Ma started to shake like a leaf and stood there looking at her with her mouth open. I held her hand and it was as cold as ice. It seemed like the longest ten minutes of my life as we stood there while Madda Penny kept on chanting and Ma stood there shaking. I tried to tell Ma to ask her if that was the interpretation of the two dreams in one but Ma didn't even feel me pulling her hand. Well, I thought I would be brave and ask Madda Penny if that was dream number one or number three, or both, but as I opened my mouth and said, 'Please, Miss Madda Penny . . .' she stood up and said, 'Leave the fee on the bench – two hundred dollars to be exact', and left. I took the money out of Ma's handbag and put it on the bench. She didn't even realise what I was doing.

If you saw Ma, you would be shocked. She was like a little child who saw a duppy. I led her to a bench under a mango tree and took her bay rum from her bag and rubbed over her face. All this time your strong strong mother was like a baby. I have never seen Ma look so helpless and frightened. Ma is not afraid of anything. She always kills the croaking lizards in my room. She moves the cows when Gramps isn't feeling well – even the big black bull. She walks home from Burial Scheme meeting by herself Tuesday night – and you remember that she has to pass by burial ground in the dark. Ma is not afraid of anything. But yesterday Ma was not the Ma that I know and I didn't like it at all.

I wish I didn't tell Ma about my dreams. If I didn't tell her she would not go to Madda Penny and we wouldn't be worrying now about this terrible warning that she gave us yesterday. Uncle Johnny is the only one who is not worried about what Madda Penny said. He says he is only sorry that Ma has taken it to heart and he hopes she doesn't send up her blood pressure and give herself a stroke over Madda Penny's warning. He says Madda Penny is not God and only God can see the future, so we must all stop this weeping weeping in the house.

Sunshine

Dear Aunt Jen,

You will get Ma's telegram before you get my letter with the terrible news I'm writing to tell you, but I still feel I must write to you. I have already written to Uncle Roy. I want to write and write and write about it because it helps me to believe that it really happened.

Uncle Johnny had an accident with the tractor yesterday. I don't know what really happened. I think something went wrong with the brakes and it turned over and pinned him down. I hear that they had to use another tractor to pull it off him and he was badly crushed from his waist down. They rushed him to the hospital and he had emergency surgery last night but he is still unconscious. I went to see him this afternoon. His face looks perfect, just as if nothing happened to him. It was so strange how he lay there as if he was just sleeping, but I could tell by the way they tied his feet to the bedposts that he is badly injured.

I felt so helpless sitting beside his bed because I wanted to do something for him but I couldn't. As I sat and looked at him lying there so still with all the tubes hanging from his body, I suddenly felt so strange and I felt like such a little dot in a big, confusing world. Uncle Johnny was a dot too, a tiny dot fighting a big big monster. I wanted to crawl into the bed and lie next to him and give him some of my strength but the nurse said I had to leave. I had your card with me and before I left I took it out of my dress pocket and put it on his chest. I wanted him to see something beautiful when he woke up. It's funny but as I left his bedside the card looked as if it was making fun of Uncle Johnny sitting there on his chest like a king using one of its subjects (a dead one) as a footstool. It looked almost as if it had a life of its own and Uncle Johnny was just a piece of furniture.

When I almost reached the end of the corridor, I ran back and took the card off his chest and put it on the table by his bed. I just didn't like the picture (which I had in my mind) of the card being more alive than Uncle Johnny.

I'm praying hard hard that he will get better soon, so he can come home. I can't imagine this house without him. Maybe this is the sudden death and destruction that Madda Penny was talking about. It's so funny, we all thought that something bad was going to happen to you. We never thought that anything would happen to Uncle Johnny.

Gramps has been in bed since the accident happened. Ma and Aunt Sue have been at the hospital since yesterday. Ma says she's not leaving until he wakes up. Uncle Roy sent a telegram to say he is going to come and see him. I think Ma is hoping that you will come too. In fact, when I told her I would write to you tonight she said to tell you to come and see your little brother now now. I think Uncle Johnny would like you to come too.

Sunshine

PS: Good news. When you come you will be able to talk to Uncle Johnny. Ma and Aunt Sue just came from the hospital and they say he woke up after I left. We are all so happy. We will go to see him tomorrow.

16 March 1971

Dear Aunt Jen,

We buried Uncle Johnny yesterday in the pouring rain. I never saw so much rain before in all my life. It came tumbling down as if somebody in the skies kicked over a big tank of water which burst through the clouds. I came out of the church while everybody was trying to get one last look at Uncle Johnny's face and by the time I realised it was raining I was already drenched. Everybody got soaking wet but nobody seemed to care. We all just wanted to be with Uncle Johnny for the last time.

I read the first lesson. Ma said that's what Uncle Johnny would want. I read from Ecclesiastes Chapter 3. I'm glad I read it because it helped a little to calm the storm inside of me, especially the part that says that there is 'a time to be born and a time to die'. I think I have to believe that it was Uncle Johnny's time to die. Uncle Johnny's season has come to an end. He no longer has a purpose here. I have to believe that but it is not so easy. I can't help thinking that Uncle Johnny still had a whole lot of things left to do.

I never saw a big funeral like that before. I haven't been to many but all the time I see many funeral processions pass by our house. Everybody in the district was there, except for Maas Bob who doesn't have any legs and Miss Dill who had a stroke last week. People came from all around, May Day, Orange Hill, Birch Hill. Some came all the way from Westmoreland where Ma is from. Some came from Clarendon where Gramps is from and Aunt Rose came with two busloads of people from Kingston. Three quarters of them stood outside the church and when we got to the burial ground they filled up all of that big big place.

Ma didn't want us to have the funeral yesterday. She said she wanted to wait until you come. Well Gramps and Uncle Roy said since we already waited for two weeks, we shouldn't wait any more. Uncle Roy says he can't understand what happened to you because when he phoned you from America you said you were definitely coming. Everybody was expecting to see you. Even when they were covering the grave we were hoping that you would turn up at the last minute to see your brother for the last time. Last night long after everybody left, Ma kept on saying, not to anyone in particular, just to herself, 'Where is Jenny? Where is Jenny? Wish-paat Jenny deh?'

Yesterday was the worst day of my life. I didn't want it to begin and when it did, I dreaded every minute. I wanted the morning to last for ever. I didn't want it to be evening because evening would mean putting Uncle Johnny in a hole in the ground and leaving him there.

When I heard that Uncle Johnny died I just felt sick. I sat on the steps and just vomited and vomited and vomited. All my feelings are knotted up in my belly bottom for two weeks. At first I thought I would die. I had a pain which felt like it started from the middle of my heart, twisted around my belly and then went down to the bottom of my feet. I really thought I would die. I never cried so much in all my life. Why did Uncle Johnny have to die before Ma and Gramps who are so old? I don't want them to die either, but Uncle Johnny was young and he was just planning to go and seek his fortune in America.

I don't think I'll ever stop missing Uncle Johnny. I miss his whistling. He could whistle the tune of any song and he did it better than when Brother Roy plays his mouth organ. I miss him begging me my dumplings. Whenever Ma made dumplings for dinner she would give him six of the biggest ones you have ever seen in your life. But he always wanted more and as soon as his eyes touched my plate, I would tell him that he could get my two dumplings if he washed the plates. He would happily wash them for dumplings. Ma used to say, 'Johnny, why you so jokify, you letting Sunshine twist you round har fingers jus fi two dumplins.' Poor Uncle Johnny. I miss his cheesy toes, I would give anything to smell his cheesy toes now. I can just picture him now – come home, sit in the kitchen, take off his shoes and bam! The smell would hit you. It was like popping open an airtight can. Sometimes I would hold my nose and run, but I'm telling you, I would give anything in the world to be near that smell now now.

Ma has taken it hard hard hard. She looks as if she added on ten years. She looks so weak and feeble. She says Johnny didn't have a long life but he had twenty-five years of love and care. He had mother-love and father-love and she knows that the mother-love was plenty plenty. She says he died with his heart full of love. But Ma says she's sure that Uncle Johnny's death was no simple simple accident. It was a hand, but she says she leaves the one who did it to God because when we get before the judgment seat every knee shall bow and every tongue shall confess. Poor Ma, I don't like to see her so sad. Every time I look at her, I want to cry again.

As to Gramps, he would have gone into the grave with Uncle Johnny if he could. He looks as if he is dead inside. He doesn't talk to anybody now. He leaves early in the morning before first cock crows and he comes back late late in the night and goes straight to bed. He doesn't even eat or smoke his pipe as before. When they were putting the coffin in the grave, Gramps threw himself on the ground and bawled. Everybody was weeping. Some women were holding up Ma and fanning her because she kept fainting – but Gramps bawled like a mad donkey braying. I will never get that picture or the sound of bawling out of my mind. Never. And I know things will never be the same again in this house for a piece of all of us went into the grave with Uncle Johnny.

I buried your card with him, for it's because of him why that card was not destroyed long ago. It's not right for it to be lying around the house while Uncle Johnny is dead and rotting in the ground. When they said 'ashes to ashes and dust to dust' and everybody was throwing dirt into the grave, I threw in the card.

Aunt Sue is staying with us for a while. I don't know what we would do without her. She cooks and runs the house for Ma because Ma seems to be in another world. Most times she just sits there like a crumpled old bag. Aunt Sue is a real rock. She knows what to do in every situation. She turned Uncle Johnny's bed upside down and she lights a candle and puts it on his chest of drawers every night. I don't think I'm going to ask her why she does it. She says tomorrow we are going to plant flowers around the grave. I think I'm going to plant some marigolds. Uncle Johnny used to pick them and put in my hair. He would like marigolds. Ma says marigold reminds her of Uncle Johnny's bright smile. She says everybody has a plant that you can match them up with. She says that for Aunt Sue it's the rose. She soft and sweet but she has macka that will jook you if you squeeze her too hard. Gramps she says is shame ol lady, for as lickle trouble touch him, him shet up. Me she says I'm periwinkle. I'm like medicine, good for her and good for Gramps. I love to listen to Ma. I always learn so much from her.

Well, we are still trying to figure out among ourselves what under God's sun could really keep you from coming to the funeral, but I hope you had a good good reason. Aunt Sue brought your sympathy card from the post office today. Ma read the little note you wrote saying that you are sorry you couldn't come to the funeral and you'll explain everything at a later date. Ma says at the rate you're going even when God come you will be makin excuses. Ma is just upset with you.

Your sympathy card reminded me of the first time you wrote to me. I was so disappointed that it was just a card that I wrote several letters to you and couldn't mail some of them because I wrote them in my anger. I even rewrote the letter I wrote to you a few weeks after because there were parts of it

30

where I knew I was really passing my place. I'm really not doing well at this waiting waiting on a letter from you.

A very disappointed Sunshine

PS: Do you know anybody else who has done anything like what you did to their family?

10 May 1971

Dear Aunt Jen,

We are all still vexed with you for not coming to Uncle Johnny's funeral, that is why I haven't written to you for such a long time. Ma says she's not writing to you but is not because cow tongue have hair why him don't talk. I don't really know what she means but when Ma talks I don't always understand.

Gramps says I'm to write because somebody has to keep in touch with you and tell you about some of the things that are happening to us. Well the first big news is that I met my father. I do not like him. I met him and grew to hate him in one week. I'll tell you more about how I came to hate him.

Now that I've met him I know what Gramps meant when he said that he's ugly. He is really ugly and I'm not talking about his buck teeth, I'm talking about the kind of person he is. I don't like the way he boasts and talks about himself all the time. The first time he came to our house he spent most of the time talking about himself and how he has got so rich since he's in England. He says he has made so much money he doesn't need to work for the rest of his life. He told us how he has so many white women running after him for his money because they like good-looking black men like him.

In the middle of his boasting Ma said dryly, 'You should

31

be givin Sunshine some ah dat money.' He looked very shocked when she said it but he forced a laugh and said, 'Of course Miss G., you know that I'm going to fix up Sunshine. I going to fix up Sunshine good good.' Ma said, 'Me hear sweeter music play an me no dance.' But my father wasn't paying Ma any mind, he said, 'That is why I'm here to talk to you about taking Sunshine to England with me. That way she will be able to enjoy my money.' Well, at that point Ma jumped up from where she was sitting and her mouth started to tremble the way it trembles when she's angry. I could see that she was trying hard hard to control her temper because the muscles in her neck and jaw were stiffening. She didn't raise her voice though, she spoke to him very quietly but the way she emphasised each word we all knew that Ma was serious serious. She looked him straight in the eyes and said, 'If and when Sunshine leave dis house it will be to go to har madda. No one else. So if yuh want har to enjoy some of yuh money, find another way to do it but yuh not teking her out of dis house.' After she hissed out those words she just flung her dress tail around and stepped off, leaving all of us staring at Mr Big Mouth Smith, who looked so shocked and confused that for one second I felt sorry for him. Gramps must have felt sorry for him too because he stood up and said, 'Well, it was good to see you again after all dese years, but it getting late. Maybe we should say goodnight now.'

Well Aunt Jen, I've never seen anyone say goodnight and goodbye so fast. He almost ran from the verandah and in two twos he was out of sight. I'm really happy that Ma spoke her mind because the more I think about it now, the more I know that I would not want to live with that man who boasts about himself so much and talks so much that nobody else can get a chance to say a word. Even if he's as rich as he says he is, I prefer to stay with Ma and Gramps and wait until you have sorted yourself out, as Uncle Roy says you're doing.

Well Aunt Jen, my father brought a few things for me and I'm telling you I never knew that such ugly things could come from England. When I think about the things you used to send for me, I can't believe it. He must have searched hard to find these ugly things. Let me tell you about them. He brought me a hat – a big broad-rimmed hat that looks like the pudding pan which Aunt Sue mixes her totoes in. He says it is the latest fashion in England now and that all the high-society ladies wear hats like it to tea parties and horse racing. I don't know how I would walk in it. I wouldn't be able to see a thing because it swallows my whole head and face when I put it on. When he left Ma said, 'Even at my ole age if I wear dis hat de whole distric would laugh me to scorn. Much more a lickle pickney like yuh. Yuh not wearing it out dis house.'

Next I have to tell you about the dress. It is fire red with about three layers of what Ma calls 'barb wire crinoline'. It just stands on me like brown paper which somebody starched. I'm sure if I walk in it, it will cut me. But the best one is the pair of shoes! He says they are mules. Ma says they're a combination of mule and jackass foot. Gramps says they are real hag head. Well, the front of them look just like Gramps' water boots except that they stick up in the air a little, and the heels look like the blocks that Maas Arthur chops up the meat in his butcher shop on. It's a good thing we didn't look at them while my father was still here because as soon as we took them out of the bag Gramps burst out laughing. It's the first I was seeing him laugh since Uncle Johnny died. He laughed and laughed until he started to cry. He said, 'Sunshine dat is what you call hag head. Ah would love to si yuh step in dem.' Well Ma was so upset she said she would tell that father of mine a piece of her mind. She says that she might be poor but she's not begging anybody anything for me – not even you. She says anybody who thinks that they can give me all kinds of old bruck that Missis

Queen don't want in England better think twice because she will not tolerate it. I haven't even seen the things since because Ma took them and hid them, but the next morning I heard her tell Aunt Sue that she's going to wrap them in a neat parcel and give them back to my father and tell him it's a little something for him to take back to England. Aunt Sue said she agrees because he should never leave England with that heng-pon-nail crocus bag frack. I would love to be there when he opens the parcel!

My father's visit was a surprise to all of us. Nobody heard anything about it. Even his mother was surprised to see him at her gate. But it seems as if he didn't want anyone to know so he just came without saying a word. Well, if we were surprised to see him that night, we were shocked when he came back the next day. We didn't think he would come back to visit us after the way Ma treated him the night before but he came again with his usual talking. He told us that he is getting married next month. He says he has found a lovely white lady who worships the very ground he walks on. Ma told him that kind of yes sar woman don't make any more and, in any case, he couldn't get married because he is still married to Jen. Well, he quickly informed her that you have been divorced for more than a year. When he saw the look of shock on Ma's face he said, 'Oh, so you didn't know that Jen is divorced and married to a white fellow from Australia?' I think he enjoyed shocking Ma because when he saw that she just stood there with her mouth open he talked and talked about you and this man. He says that the man is very bossy and he controls you. He doesn't know about me because you are afraid of him and you don't want him to know about your bastard pickney in Jamaica. He says he thought of telling the man himself but he decided to stay out of your life. 'Miss G.,' he said, 'if fish come up from ribber battam and say alligetta dung deh wid sore mout, believe him.'

Ma looked at him like she wanted to dig out his eyes and

said, 'You could never be calling Sunshine a bastard.' Then she just got up and went to her room and locked the door. I was so disappointed that she didn't get a chance to tell him about the ugly things he brought for me. Gramps just sat there puffing and puffing away at his pipe. Of course, since neither Ma nor Gramps seems to want to talk about the matter I cannot even mention it. But I have been thinking about it a lot. I realise now that you are even more of a stranger to me than I have been thinking. I don't know anything about you. Why didn't you tell us about your divorce? Are you really married again? Is this why you won't write to us or reply to my letters? Was Madda Penny right when she said there's a man in your life who rules you? What other important information are you keeping from us? Is that why you stopped writing to Ma? What is going on in your life?

The more I think about it now the more I wonder if I really want to get to know you or be involved with you. Maybe when I finally meet you I will grow to dislike you soon after, just like my father. I'm telling you I'm really confused about you. You are like a big jigsaw puzzle which I don't think I'll ever be able to put together.

All this time we have been here worrying about you and believing like Uncle Roy that you're just sorting yourself out when you have been keeping secrets from us. I think I let Ma put too many ideas of going to live with my mother in my head. Maybe I should forget this dream. It's just that it is a little difficult for me to understand how you could sit in England all these years and not even send a photograph so I can see what you look like. Why don't you want me to see what you look like? I tell you, my life is really interesting. I have a mother somewhere in England who will not reply to my letters and a father I met and hated in the space of one week.

I should tell you what caused me to really hate him. The

third time he came to our house he asked Ma if I could spend some time with him. Ma was not too happy about the idea but she said I could go for a little while. Well, when I got to my other grandmother's house where he was staying, he had taken out three pairs of shoes – dirty, muddy shoes which he said he wanted me to clean. I told him I don't clean people's shoes. I just said it straight out because I never cleaned Ma's or Gramps' or Uncle Johnny's shoes. Well he got angry and used one of the same dirty shoes to give me the biggest beating I ever have in my life. When I went and told Ma she took all the things he brought for me and gave them back to him. She told him to tek his hurry come up langulala self go back to England with his old bruck and his damn facety English idea about me cleaning his shoes and leave me out of his life. She said he should go back to England and find some white slave woman if is slave he lookin. Gramps told him that if he wants to go back to England in one piece he must not put his hands on me again. I tell you I hated him for beating me like that. Do you know that in all these years Gramps and Uncle Johnny never lifted a hand to hit me? So if that man only just met me and beats me to clean his dirty shoes I can imagine that he would really want me to be his little slave if I went to live with him in England. I don't want to see him again.

If at all at all you find it possible to reply, please do. I think you owe Ma and Gramps an explanation. Your secret is out now anyway. So please write to them before you kill them off.

Sunshine

PS: Aunt Sue says she will put her head on de block fe yuh. She know that yuh would never get married and not tell the family. Well, this is your chance to prove if she's right or wrong about you.

25 May 1971

Dear Aunt Jen,

     I'm so used to not getting a reply to my letters that I don't even bother to wait on you any more. I think part of the reason for that is because I don't talk to the hibiscus hedge so much these days so I write to you instead. You are not really different from the hibiscus hedge, even though you are a person, because just as how it just listens, you just sit in England and never reply. I think though that I prefer to write more than I like to talk these days, so I write to you. Sometimes I think that one day I'll get a big big parcel from the post office with all my letters to you coming back unopened. I usually think that when I'm trying to figure out what could be keeping you from writing to me.

             I am very puzzled,
                 Sunshine

PS: Uncle Roy says he doesn't believe you are married. He says my father is just trying to cause trouble. Gramps says the man doesn't have any reason to tell that kind of lie. Ma still has not said a word about it. We are waiting to hear from you.

31 May 1971

Dear Aunt Jen,

     I am feeling a little depressed this week. I don't think it's because I'm thinking about Uncle Johnny although he is always on my mind. I think I'm a little sad that so many of my friends are leaving. Last month Maxine went to her mother in America.

Last week Yvonne and Sharon went to England to their parents and yesterday my best friend Joan went to England to her mother. At first I thought I was sad because I'm envious of them, but the more I think about it the more I know that I'm not envious, I'm just a little sad that all these people who are going to England could get to know you before I even see a photograph of you. I don't want to leave Jamaica like my friends. I like my life with Ma and Gramps. I like sitting on the back steps in the sun in the mornings. I like to watch the mongooses dodging in and out of Gramps' callaloo and dasheen beds. I like to watch Ma's chickens walking in the yard and wonder which one Ma is going to cook next. No, I am not envious. I just want a letter and a photograph of you. Furthermore, I hear that England is cold cold cold and everybody is always cold. I'll miss my friends, but I'll stay right here with Ma and Gramps.

Sunshine

10 June 1971

Dear Aunt Jen,

So many things are going through my mind that I feel I have to write to somebody and talk about them. I am still waiting on my friends to write to me and Uncle Roy already knows about these things so you are really the only person I can write to now. Ma says the truth of the matter is that I'm looking for an excuse to write to you.

I think that Flour Hill is changing. It is not just because Uncle Johnny died or because my friends went away. It's all the many other terrible things that have suddenly started to happen, just like the whole place is turning upside down. Ma says is jus a time of tribulation that is on us and it will soon pass. I hope she's right because we can't take any more of these things much longer. Ma says it started with Uncle Johnny's death and she hopes to Almighty God it will not end with another young life. It too hard and sorrowful.

It is really true that some of the strangest and most terrible things that happen in Flour Hill happen since Uncle Johnny died. Last week Wednesday Maas Beres' bull ran him down and almost bucked him to death. It ripped off all his clothes. Maas Beres had to run naked as the day he was born from all the way over Cane straight to his house. Ma says she has never seen anything like that in all her days on this earth. She says is a shame because Maas Beres is such a nice, humble man and he doesn't deserve to suffer such a disgrace. That same evening Maas Beres sent for Mr Whitelocke with his gun and they shot the bull. Maas Beres says he could never keep an animal like that for one more day. We hardly see him these days. People say he hasn't got over the shame. Gramps says he should jus laugh about the whole thing now and forget it or shame will kill him if he takes it so serious. Ma says Gramps can talk because it didn't happen to him. I believe it must be a hard hard shock to get over, so I think I understand how Maas Beres feels.

I know I didn't tell you about Miss Jane because it happened so soon after Uncle Johnny died. I was so sad about Uncle Johnny I didn't really think about poor Miss Jane. Ma says you used to like Miss Jane because she used to bring tamarind balls and stewed June plums for you every time she made them. She says she doesn't know why but Miss Jane had a special special liking for you because one time she even gave you a white rooster that you always used to love. She used to ask for you all the time and Ma says she always tells her that you send howdy-do for her even when you didn't mention her, because she said is a shame that you don't seem to remember somebody who was so good to you.

Well you will be shocked to know that Miss Jane burnt up in her bed. People say she was reading her Bible with the lamp in the bed, fell asleep and the lamp turn over, catch the bed a-fire and burn her up. They say Miss Jane burn she burn she burn she burn to nothing. Miss Lize says, in all her eighty odd years she never see anything like it where somebody jus burn like paper or wood.

As if Miss Jane's death was not bad enough, the night of her nine night Raleigh, who was the main gravedigger for Uncle Johnny's grave, dropped out of Miss Jane's breadfruit tree and broke his two legs. He's still in hospital with his feet tied to the bedposts – at least that is what I hear. Ma says he's lucky because bruk up bone better than death.

Well Miss Jane's death was awful, the bull chasing was disgraceful and Raleigh's situation was bad (although Ma says it was also kind of funny because he was out of order to be in the breadfruit tree in the middle of the night picking what don't belong to him). But when I tell you what happened yesterday in Flour Hill I think you will be shocked shocked. In fact I think you will jump on the next plane to come and find out what is going on in your district and make sure you see your old parents before anything happens to them (or me).

Yesterday evening was Miss Clara's daughter's funeral – Miss Clara from Bowen's Pasture, not Miss Clara from Cross Roads. We are not so sure what happened but she went to Lucea to have her baby and died before the baby was born. Anyway, yesterday when they were marching with her body from the Salvation Army church to the burial ground, the funeral car got out of control as it was coming down the hill and crashed into the big plum tree at our gate. It crashed into the tree so hard that the coffin flew right out of it and landed on its side in the middle of the gate. The dropping was bad enough but when the coffin burst open at the sides everybody started to scream and shout. Some started to run and Major Rankine started to shout, 'Demons of hell! Demons of hell! Be gone with you!' She shouted even louder when all kinds of things started to tumble out of the coffin – scissors, broom, needle and thread, baby nappy, baby bottle, baby pin, olive oil, vials with other oils and a whole heap of other things that I couldn't make out. When the things stopped tumbling out everybody just stopped bawling and screaming at the same time. Everybody stood there waiting to see if the body would drop out too. When they waited for about a half a minute and nothing happened Miss Clara threw herself on the ground and started to roll and bawl. Some men ran and lifted up the coffin and started to push back the things into it. Major Rankine said, 'Sweet Jesus, resurrector of Lazarus, what is this? Deliver us from the enemy's trap. Demons of hell be gone!' Well it seems as if Major Rankine's teeth couldn't take the pressure any more so by the time she started to say 'Gone' again, the teeth flew right out of her mouth and landed on the pile of things that dropped out of the coffin. I thought Major Rankine would run and grab them up, but instead she just pulled up her white Salvation Army uniform above her knee and ran and ran shouting, 'Thave me Jesus, thave me!' I don't think any of us could catch her at the speed she was going.

Some people ran into our house and Ma shouted, 'Don't tek it in dere at all at all.' Miss Clara's husband picked her up off the ground and told her to stop disgracing herself and let them hurry up and finish off with the funeral. When they scraped up everything and put it into the coffin they put back the coffin in the car and about ten men decided to push the car straight to burial ground. They didn't take out Major Rankine's teeth though. The Lieutenant said, 'Ladies and gentlemen, let us be calm. This is a terrible terrible thing that has happened but the devil must not have his way. We are going to give this young lady a decent burial. Cease the weeping and wailing and let us sing, "We are marching to Zion", until we get to the burial ground.'

Well, Ma took off her hat and gloves and said not a funeral for her. Aunt Sue joined in with her and the two of them went and got kerosene oil, matches, white rum, salt and Ma's bottle of Good Friday water and they sprinkled the whole place where the accident happened and then they set it on fire. Ma says she doesn't want any more trial and crosses in her yard. She doesn't want any evil from those things to follow us. When all the grass on the area finished burning Aunt Sue went to her house for incense and lit it in an Ovaltine tin and walked round and round the house with it.

It is the most horrible thing I've seen in all my life. I thought that coffins only had the dead body in them. Ma says that's how it should be but some people have all kinds of stupid ideas about different things that they should put in it with the dead person. She says that when she was a girl if a woman died in childbirth it meant that she died unhappy so they would give her all the baby's things and other things to keep her busy so she wouldn't come back and look for the baby. She said she didn't know that people still do those things but that is how life is. She says Miss Clara is not upset that the coffin drop, she jus shame that everybody find out what she did in secret. She said I must take it as a warning that everything done in darkness will come to light one way or another. She says in Miss Clara's case, she is a big big Christian who goes to church every Sunday speaking in tongues and casting out demons, so after all and after all she has no business getting mix up mix up in that kind of thing. She says those things are from the world of darkness and Christian people must stay away from them. Well, I was a little confused so I asked Ma if the sprinkling and burning that she and Aunt Sue did were not from the world of darkness too, but she said not at all at all, that was just chasing away evil. I told her I thought we should pray to chase away evil and she said yes of course you pray but you do those things too to help the prayer.

I hope this letter will help me to get that awful picture out of my mind. Usually writing helps me to stop thinking so much about things. Last night I didn't sleep because I just kept seeing the things fall out one by one from the coffin. Ma says the worse part about it is that it happened at her gate as if she don't have enough worries in her life. If Uncle Johnny was alive he would laugh so much about the whole thing. Gramps says he doesn't know how Clara will live down this one for it worse dan Maas Beres' disgrace. I'm just hoping I'll forget about it soon soon because I need to sleep at nights.

Write and tell me what you think about all these things. I'm sure this doesn't sound like the Flour Hill that you know.

I am anxious,

Sunshine

PS: I'm telling you Aunt Jen, if all these changes continue like this the whole place will be strange strange when you come.

30 June 1971

Dear Aunt Jen,

Today I sat and thought about you for a long, long time. I thought about how strange it is that you're my mother and I am your daughter and you are there and I am here and we don't know each other and if I came to England or if you came to Jamaica we would pass each other on the streets and you would not know me and I would not know you ... We would pass each other and not know that we are flesh and blood. That is really strange.

I tried to picture you sitting in your house in England. I can barely see a body. Maybe it's a body like Ma's, only a little younger. Maybe it's a body like mine, only older. It's very hard to see a picture of you in my mind. I can't see a face. I tried to imagine the face of a lady who looks like Uncle Roy and Uncle Johnny but it's not working. I tried to picture a lady who looks like me, as Uncle Eddy said, but that does not work either. It's like trying to see my own face in a dirty mirror. I'm still hoping you will send me a photograph of yourself.

~~Your daughter~~

~~Your dau~~

Sunshine

15 October 1971

Dear Aunt Jen,

Gramps says I'm to write and tell you that you spreading you bed hard hard with the family. He says if you don't change your ways, shape up and keep in touch with us, you going to reap what you sow. He says I'm to write it exactly the way he says it.

I don't know why he doesn't write and tell you himself. Maybe if you got a letter from him you would reply to him. Anyway, when Gramps starts to talk, you know that things are bad bad, for Gramps does not talk or interfere in anything that's happening in the house. He gets up in the morning and goes to look after his yams, his rice and his animals. He comes home late in the evenings, eats, smokes his pipe, goes to bed after the eight o'clock news. He sleeps, wakes up next morning and leaves. That is his daily pattern. But your behaviour has been so strange that not even Gramps can ignore it. Can you imagine that Gramps is now talking about going to Madda Penny himself to see if she can tell him anything about you?

I think that he's secretly wondering if my third dream means that another terrible tragedy is going to happen in the family. Your silence and all this news about you being married has added to his confusion and concern about what is happening in your life. You have become a real mystery to all of us. Ma and Gramps are worried because they don't like the secrecy. Aunt Sue says you must really be hiding something. She can't believe you could be so hard to keep everybody guessin an speculatin. I don't know what to think. I was curious about you at first but now I am not sure it makes sense to continue to write to someone who never replies. Sometimes I don't agree with Aunt Sue that you must have a good reason for not writing. Please excuse me for saying so but sometimes I think it takes a hard, cold person to behave the way you are. Sometimes I get really angry with you. Sometimes I feel like I would rip you to pieces just like the letters.

Let me give you a little piece of advice. Try not to let Ma wash her hands of you. I heard her telling Aunt Sue that anyhow she decides to wash her hands of you – you could be dead, alive or ailing jt will not matter at all at all to her. She's serious. Write to her before things get to that stage.

Sunshine

PS: 'Tek mi foolish advice,' as Ma would say.

Dear Aunt Jen,

When I started writing to you I thought it would be the beginning of a meaningful relationship in which we – me and you – would exchange pleasant, enjoyable and interesting letters on a regular basis. It was not my idea that I would be the only one writing and I certainly didn't think I would end up just writing to relay Ma's and Gramps' messages. But unfortunately, due to no fault of my own, this is what is happening. I have now become the scribe of two parents who feel neglected by a daughter for whom they scraped up every last penny so that she could make a better life for herself in England.

So this is a brief letter which I am writing for Ma. She says she needs to know if she is to give me to my father or not. She says that since you are not writing and she hear that you married to man who don't want no bastard, she wants to know if it is all right for me to go to live with my father. Now that I am writing it, I feel like a real little goat that can be passed from one owner to another. I don't believe that Ma means it. I think she just wants to make you feel bad. In any case, Ma has always said I am not going anywhere until her eyes shut so I don't think she means it, but I'm writing what she says.

As much as I hate being treated as if I'm up for raffle, I'm writing Ma's message. I don't know why she thinks that this will make you write. I don't know *what* will make you write.

Sunshine

Dear Aunt Jen,

I've finally had another dream about you! I haven't dreamt about you since I had those three strange dreams I told you about. Don't think that I haven't been dreaming. I dream all the time but not about you. Most of the times I have these strange dreams that don't seem to have any end. Sometimes a cow is running me down. Sometimes I'm in the middle of the road and a big truck is coming and I can't move. But last night you were in my dreams. It's like you came back from a long holiday outside of my dream-world. It was a long dream that went on almost all night.

First I dreamt that you came and you brought a baby. The baby's skin was smooth and soft and you had him in your arms all the time. You wouldn't allow a soul to touch him. You just kept rocking him and singing to him. I can hear your voice even now hush du-du:

> Don't cry, don't cry
> Till mama come home
> Mama bring bun for baby alone
> Baby eat bun, no give nursey none
> Nursey get vex an throw baby down.

You sang it over and over and over. I thought the baby was asleep because he wasn't making a sound. But he suddenly burst out bawling. He started a cow bawling as Ma would put it. It was such a shock that the baby was so still and then suddenly he just started bawling and bawling. I was so frightened I jumped up out of my sleep.

In the second part of the dream everything changed. You weren't here but you were in England and I got a letter from you with a photograph. I just remember holding it and thinking

47

that after all this time of begging and begging for a photograph you finally sent it. Well, by now you should know that any dream with you in it must have some strange things happening in it. So let me tell you what else happened in this dream. I took the photograph to school the next day and showed it to my friends. I wanted them to see what my mother looks like. When they looked at it they all had a funny look on their faces and then Marva said, 'Sunshine, I don't see nobody in this picture. Is a blank piece a paper.'

I grabbed the paper from them thinking that they were all crazy. I looked at the paper and saw Ma's face looking back at me. I was shocked and confused and embarrassed. I wanted to say something but not a sound would come out of my mouth. My friends were standing there just looking at me as if I was mad mad mad. I started to run because I didn't want to look at them. I tripped on a stone and fell but I jumped up and continued to run. I was washing in cold sweat when I jumped up out of my sleep. I felt so confused by these two strange dreams that I couldn't sleep for the rest of the night.

I've been thinking about those dreams all day but I am not going to mention a word about them to Ma. She would just start to fret, especially since I saw her face in the photograph. I don't want to know what those dreams mean so after I finish your letter I'm just going to put them out of my mind.

I don't even know why I'm telling you because nothing seems to matter to you at all at all at all.

Sunshine

Dear Aunt Jen,

I just hit upon a great great idea. I think it would be a wonderful idea for you to come to Jamaica for Christmas. You would make Ma and Gramps happy happy. I can see their faces now. They would laugh and laugh and behave as if they turn fool fool. Gramps would just walk around grinning and grinning and saying, 'Sunshine me glad bag burst, chile.' You wouldn't have to bring a thing for them. Just the sight of you would be enough for them. Ma wouldn't eat a thing. She would just sit down and sigh and say over and over, 'Jen come. Jen come.' I think it is definitely a good idea and if you decide to come I will not tell a soul. It would be our secret. So, let's plan everything and give Ma and Gramps the best Christmas present of their lives. I'm excited just to think about it.

I really got this idea when I went to see Major Critchlow yesterday. I don't know if you remember her, but she used to tell me that she taught you in Sunday school and she always remembers how your eyes used to be big and bright and shine.

I used to like Major Critchlow. She used to tell me a lot of stories and she always said that I must always mind my p's and q's. She went back to Gibraltar about four years ago. She said she was old and tired and it was time for some younger Caribbean people to do the work of the Salvation Army in the island.

Major Critchlow came back to Flour Hill last week. She said she wanted to see all the people she left here before she's too old and shaky to travel. Everybody was happy to see her. Uncle Eddy says she looks exactly the same as when she left Flour Hill four years ago. He says sometimes he has to wonder if she is really ninety-two, as she says.

I was surprised to see her too. She walks strong strong like

49

any young person. When she saw me, she hugged me tight tight tight and squeezed me and said, 'Oh Sunshine my dear. You've grown to be such a beautiful young lady. I wish your mother could see you now! Is she coming for Christmas? She should come to see you. It really would be nice if she came for Christmas.' That was when I said I should make this suggestion to you.

Christmas is my favourite time of year. Well, I should explain that I like the food, the new clothes, the decorations and all the presents that I get. I don't like the work though. Every year, just before Christmas, Ma turns into a slave driver. When Gramps asks her why she has to work so hard for one day, she says it's the best day of the year and it can only be good if we all work hard to get everything perfect. Ma says no music is sweeter to the ears than a Christmas carol and she says that somehow on Christmas Day Parson just suddenly seems to find something sensible to preach about. Gramps says he doesn't know about the carols but church is the best part of Christmas Day because all he does is to find a corner, put his hat over his head and sleep. That is the last day of the year when he gets a good sleep in church because the carols are just like lullabys. Ma says as long as he makes sure that when the trumpet blows he can hear, that is all right. Well Gramps always says the only thing that matters to him is that she doesn't control his eating and drinking on that day. He says from it touches December he has no say in what he does, how he does it or when he does it. Ma has a whole string of things for him to do. Cut the sorrel, pick the sorrel, dig the ginger, chop wood for the brick oven, kill the pig, kill the goat, hang up the curtains, paint the gate, whitewash the trees, paint the walls, clean his shoes, wash his hair, clean his finger nails.

Anyway, I think that Gramps is planning to rebel this Christmas because the other night I heard him telling Ma that

50

by hook or by crook this Christmas is going to be different from all the others. He says he just wants a quiet season. He cannot take this whole month of working himself to death for one day. He said that Ma must understand that this year he plans to eat like a man and he's not going to put up with just the three glasses of sorrel and two one-sided slice of cake that Ma always measures out to him every year after he works so hard to provide the things. Tups of this, tups of that, sample of this, sample of that. He says he doesn't know why Ma thinks that every Christmas she must feed the whole district. He says his mouth barely tastes the sorrel that he plants and picks and as to the pork and mutton, Ma just offers him a little piece because she has to make sure that everybody in Flour Hill eats pig's tail stew and curried goat for Christmas. Well Ma told him that he must stop carrying on because she never see any three-hundred-tail pig kill in this yard.

After that Ma just let Gramps talk and talk and talk. She didn't say another word to him. I think that Ma knows deep in her heart that Gramps is not really mean and selfish and I know that Gramps is just teasing Ma to get her to talk and stop thinking so much about Uncle Johnny. Gramps doesn't like to see Ma so quiet. Gramps doesn't really mind when she shares our food with other people in Flour Hill. He knows that Ma's philosophy is always that we cannot sit and eat on Christmas Day while other people have nothing. That is not the Christian way, Ma says.

To tell you the truth, I understand what Gramps is saying about the work though, because every Christmas I work and work and work until I feel sorry for myself. Ma cleans and washes every single thing in the house and I have to work toe to toe with her. Ma sews new curtains for every window and I have to hem every one of them. (Gramps says what a day that was when he brought that sewing machine from Panama.) Last year I told Ma I could practise my stitching on the machine with the curtains but she said not at all at all. She says hemming with my hands is what I must learn to do properly. She said a young lady who cannot do a neat neat hem is no young lady at all. She said the machine is almost the same age as you and older than Uncle Johnny for sure and about three times my age. She says I must plain and simple use my hands that the good Lord gave me. To tell you the truth, it is all this Christmas working that made me change my mind about crocheting. Just as Aunt Sue started teaching me to crochet, Ma said, 'Well Sunshine, Christmas you can do some nice pieces for all the tables and bureaus in the house.' Well, when I thought of all the tables and bureaus that Ma has, I decided that I wouldn't learn to crochet again so Ma wouldn't have a reason to force me to make about a dozen pieces of crochet every Christmas. I told Aunt Sue that I didn't really like crocheting any more. She said it was strange how I changed my mind sudden sudden so, but I didn't explain anything to her.

Then there is the baking. Ma and Aunt Sue bake totoes, puffs and puddings. Uncle Johnny used to say they could feed the world and his wife with all the things they bake. (I'm going to miss Uncle Johnny so much this Christmas.)

Two nights before Christmas Eve I always burn the midnight oil because I have to rub the butter and sugar until they are smooth like Pond's Cream, according to Ma. Sometimes I rub and rub and rub until I feel like my hand is going to drop off. The only good part about it was that Uncle Johnny and I always hid and ate it. (Uncle Johnny was like a real little child with that.)

The day before Christmas Eve is always baking day. Ma says you used to love that day because you love Christmas cake. Every year I work so hard on that day I always go to my bed early. The heat from the oven makes me so hot and tired that I

52

always wonder how Aunt Sue and Ma can push their head in the oven for so long and come out with hair on their head. They are strong for their age. Last year when Aunt Sue was there peeping in the oven at the cakes, a little wicked thought flashed through my mind. I remembered the old witch in the story about Hansel and Gretel and I wondered what would happen if I just push her in the oven and roast her like Hansel and Gretel did with the witch. Anyway, I was shocked when I realised what I was thinking and quickly rebuked the devil for putting that thought in my innocent mind. Aunt Sue is not even anything like a witch.

Well, I was telling you how I work and work and work for Christmas every year and then, just like Gramps was complaining how Ma gives away everything, on Christmas Day I have to walk the whole of Flour Hill with cake, sorrel, puffs and totoes for everybody. Sometimes I want to just sit down and eat off the whole tray of things and then go back home. But I know that Ma would figure it out when Miss so or so and Maas so and so don't come and tell her thanks for the Christmas things and I wouldn't want to face that music. So I make trip after trip delivering Ma's presents. I don't want you to think that I don't like Christmas. I love it. I love when the Salvation Army people wake us up early in the morning with their carolling. I love to eat all the different Christmas foods although sometimes, most of the times, I agree with Gramps that everybody else in Flour Hill gets most of the food. I wish Ma would leave a little more for us.

Of course, Gramps is just full of talk and as much as he thinks he has an axe to grind, I know that when the time comes for him to work this Christmas season, he will just eat humble pie. When Ma says cut the sorrel and dig the ginger he will just jump up and say, 'How much?' But you know that even if Gramps cannot make this Christmas different by refusing to work, you can make it different for him, if you come for Christmas. I think the only thing that could make Ma behave differently this Christmas is the pain she still feels about Uncle Johnny. Nothing else.

Hurry and write and tell me what you decide. You know you are the apple of Gramps' and Ma's eyes, so please come. I won't let the cat out of the bag. I think you still have time to book a flight and come.

Sunshine

PS: If you find it hard to make up your mind, just think about Maas Cleve's cane juice, Ma's pig trotters, roast pork and run down, her rice and peas with real real coconut milk, Miss Todd's totoes and Aunt Sue's gizadas. Think about Ma's ginger beer and Christmas cake, a big glass of sorrel with a little tups of Gramps' real real Jamaican spirits. I don't think I need to mention the poinsettias. . . .

20 January 1972

Dear Aunt Jen,

Christmas came and went and the New Year is twenty days old now and not a word from you. Every day I get up and just think about how you didn't come for Christmas. You didn't come. You didn't come. You didn't come. You did not come. You are a hard person.

Sunshine

Dear Aunt Jen,

I'm in a good mood today, at least I'm feeling better than the last time I wrote to you. Of course my good mood has nothing to do with you because nothing has changed where you are concerned. I write. You read my letters. You fold them and put them away or maybe you tear them up and throw them in the garbage. I don't know what you do with them and I'm not so sure that it really matters now.

Let me tell you why I'm in a good mood. I just got my report and I finally beat Milton and Jimmy in math. I came first as usual. Of course you wouldn't know that I always come first in my class. But I always wanted to beat those two ugly boys in math. (They're not really ugly. They are just full of themselves.) I always beat them in all the other subjects and I've been longing to beat them in math by even one mark. Well I whipped them good and proper this time. Even I have to admit though that they are very good at math. But I think that their marks have been going down because they are so taken up with politics these days. They spend most of their time discussing the election which is going to happen soon.

Well all of us talk about it a lot and we can't help it because all the teachers encourage us to talk about the elections in class and everywhere you go now people are talking about it. Most of us in my age group understand what an election is about for the first time and I think that is why Milton and Jimmy are so excited.

At first, Ma and Gramps and I were not paying much attention to it because of Uncle Johnny's death. But everybody talks about it so much now that Gramps started talking about it too. Uncle Eddy used to talk and talk to Gramps about it because he says it is the most exciting election that he can remember. I think all the old people like the excitement that this person that most people say will be the next prime minister is creating. He calls himself 'Joshua' so everywhere you turn now that is all you hear – 'Joshua is the Leader'. Of course in Flour Hill and Lucea too you have people who say they still want the same prime minister. They say they know him and they prefer to stick with the evil that they know rather than swap black dog for monkey. But Uncle Eddy says there's nobody else for him but Joshua because the word is love. Uncle Eddy walks around with his rod these days. He says it is the rod of correction like Joshua's rod. Nowadays, Gramps gives me money to buy the *Gleaner* for him when I go to school in Lucea because he has to read about what Joshua said at his political meetings. Since Uncle Johnny died this is the only thing that has really made him get a little excited. Maybe he's using it to take his mind off Uncle Johnny.

But Ma is still only thinking about Uncle Johnny and she says she doesn't see what the excitement is all about. Aunt Sue says she agrees with Ma and she doesn't like all this talk about 'The word is love'. She says when people talk about love love love all the time like that, they could be real jinnals. Ma says maybe they not jinnals but they don't need to talk so much about love – they must just act. Action she says speaks louder than words. Furthermore Ma says this word is love thing just put her in mind of Mrs Delgado's sons. One day I will really have to find out this thing about Mrs Delgado's sons because every once in a while Ma mentions it but I don't really know the story.

Well, I think a lot of people – even Milton and Jimmy – are excited for the wrong reasons. I think they like this man because he is such a good talker. He can talk and talk for hours without stopping. His voice is powerful and almost magical. You could sit and listen to him for hours without getting bored.

He's a good speaker. People love that. They love to hear him say the same things over and over for ten times and they get excited. But I think Gramps is wise. I started to study the history of Jamaica since Independence and I agree with Gramps that maybe it is time to try a new kind of politics. Gramps says we need new people and new plans. I agree. Well, Ma says she is a Labourite from the days of the Chief and she has no intentions of changing now. She says no other leader is as good as the Chief – and anyway, she says not a new leader and not a rod of correction can bring back Johnny and that is all that matters to her right now. Gramps says he's still grieving for Johnny but election is a big big thing and it seems as if Labour really going to lose for the first time at last so we have to talk about it.

Anyway, I was telling you about Milton and Jimmy and how all they talk about these days is Joshua and how Joshua going to change things for people like us. They go to political meetings all over the place. I think they have decided that they want to become politicians. Well, when I saw that they were missing classes sometimes and that their mind is not really on school work, I realised it was my chance to work harder at the math that they always beat me at. It worked. So I'm just feeling on top of the world now.

Anyway, I must be a real coco-head because I don't know why I keep telling you the things that are important to me. I should go back to the hibiscus hedge.

Sunshine

5 February 1972

Dear Aunt Jen,

I sat and watched a worm crawling along this morning. At first he didn't really seem to be able to decide where he was going, but after crawling around a bit he suddenly seemed to decide on the direction he wanted to take. I watched him for a long, long time as he kept going and going and going in that direction. It seemed as if that was the only thing on his mind. Lucky him. I wish I could be like him and not have so many things on my mind.

One of the things I have on my mind is Ma. I'm worried about her. Yesterday I looked at her and I suddenly realised that she has got old old. I know she was always old but I think she has added on ten years since Uncle Johnny died. She looks like a long, tired lizard walking on two legs and her eyes are sad and colourless. I can't remember the last time I heard her sing. In fact I don't think I've heard her sing since Uncle Johnny died. She spends a lot of time in her bedroom these days and she doesn't say much to anyone – not even to Aunt Sue. She doesn't even look at Uncle Eddy when he's carrying on about Joshua these days. Before, she used to tell him that he's behaving like he's stone drunk but now she just looks straight through him. Aunt Sue says we have to understand that Uncle Johnny's death was a real shock and a blow, so Ma needs a good year or two before she will stop grieving and be herself again. Aunt Sue says Ma has a lot burdening her because in addition to mourning for Uncle Johnny she has to deal with your out-of-order behaviour. She says you're behaving as if you want to send your mother to her grave.

Anyway, Ma has always been strong, stronger than Gramps. Gramps is the one who is always complaining about his back or his arthritis or his bad foot or something and Ma

58

has to take care of him. I hope she will soon start looking again like the Ma that I know and get back to weeding her garden, cooking and going to church and fussing around the house. The house is just not the same when Ma is quiet.

I went to look at Uncle Johnny's grave today. The marigolds are blooming. They are a golden yellow that reminds me of Uncle Johnny's happy face and his big, broad grin. It is their season to live and flourish on my uncle's grave.

I think that Ma goes to the grave every day. I know she goes every Saturday and Sunday when I'm here. She just stands there for a long long time and stares and stares at the grave and then she goes back to her room. Poor Ma, I wish I could help her.

Maybe you could write a little letter to her and see if that will help to cheer her up. It's up to you – I'm just making a suggestion.

Sunshine

PS: Isn't it funny that Ma is pining so much after her dead son and you don't even seem to want to know your daughter who is alive.

29 February 1972

Dear Aunt Jen,

Gramps ordered me to write to you immediately, whether I want to or not, and tell you about Ma. So, please understand that I am just following Gramps' orders. Ma is in the hospital. We had to take her there yesterday.

I found her lying on the kitchen floor when I went to get my breakfast. I thought she was dead because when I put my head to her chest I didn't hear a sound. I got so frightened, I just heard myself screaming for Gramps. But even if I screamed with all my might Gramps couldn't hear because he was down at Cornlands looking after his animals. I ran all the way down to Aunt Sue's house screaming and hollering for her.

When she heard me she just dropped the eggs that she had in her hands and ran back with me. I didn't even think that she could run. Aunt Sue was shocked when she saw Ma lying so still on the floor. She started screaming: 'Gertie, Gertie! Yuh dead! Yuh dead! Oh God, oh God!' Then she said, 'Come Sunshine we have to get yuh granmadda in de bed.'

Ma was like a cloth-dolly when we lifted her. Her arms just dropped and dangled like long strings at her sides. I can't believe that Ma has really got so thin. When we put her in the bed Aunt Sue said, 'Pass mi a looking glass Sunshine, ah want to se if she still blowing.' After she held the mirror to Ma's face for a while she said, 'Praise God, Gertie no dead. Sunshine, run go call you granfada.'

I've never run so fast in all my life. When Gramps saw me he said, 'But Sunshine you getting off you head. Why you not gone to school?' When I told him what had happened, he dropped everything and said, 'Come, you can't walk no more. Come on de donkey wid me.' That was my first donkey ride and to tell you the truth, under normal circumstances I would not go on that bony backed Mavis with Gramps, but I felt as if I would collapse if I took another step.

Well, I've never heard Gramps quarrel with Mavis so much. The donkey just could not walk fast or lift up her half-dead mawga foot dem fast enough for Gramps and he kept shouting, and coaxing and calling her all kinds of lazy names.

When we got to the house Gramps just jumped off the donkey and left me there wondering what to do. Anyway, I managed to slide down and ran into the house behind Gramps.

Aunt Sue had already called some of the neighbours and told them that Ma drop down so the room was full of people. Gramps just kept pushing them out of the way and shouting, 'Call Missa Mack! Call Missa Mack! Somebody go get Missa Mack taxi. We have to get Gertie to de hospital!'

Everything happened so fast. I don't even remember when the car came or how they got Ma into it. I just remember it speeding off fast fast and hearing Gramps shout, 'Sunshine, don't go to school today. Stay till ah come back.'

I didn't want to go to school anyway. I wanted to go to the hospital and be with Ma. I didn't feel like crying, I just felt nervous nervous nervous. I was not hungry so I didn't eat a thing. While I was waiting Uncle Eddy came to find out if they came back from the hospital yet. He showed me his finger with the red ink – that was when I remembered that it was election day. In all the confusion about Ma everybody forgot about the elections. Uncle Eddy started to sing 'You wrong fe trouble Joshua, you wrong. For Joshua is a lion and lion will devour you . . .' I said, 'Uncle Eddy, Joshua may be your lion, but Ma is my lion and I hope she will be a lion against this sickness now.' He laughed and said, 'Sunshine, you start sounding like you granmadda.' When he left I just sat on the verandah and waited all day until Gramps and Aunt Sue came back.

They said that the doctors didn't really explain anything to them. They just kept saying that they shouldn't worry and that Ma will soon be fine. Gramps says the doctors think he doesn't have brain to understand what is wrong but they better make sure nothing happen to Ma because it won't end simple simple so.

Last night the house felt so empty. Even though Ma was spending so much time in her room these days, I still missed her. I always felt happy once Ma was in the house. I hope the doctors are right because neither Gramps nor I could live without Ma. Ma cannot die like Uncle Johnny. Ma has to come home to cook and wash and iron and pray for us and talk to us and talk to Aunt Sue and clean Gramps' pipe and listen to us and tell us to go to church and go to Uncle Johnny's grave and worry about you and tell me that one day you will shape up and start to treat me right.

I went to see her in the hospital today. She just lay there like she was sleeping. I touched her and she didn't even budge. I didn't like the way she looked. It was just like the day I went to see Uncle Johnny. It was the same thing all over again. I was just standing there, looking at her, feeling frightened and confused, I really didn't know what to think – she wasn't sleeping and she wasn't dead but she didn't look like she would wake up soon. I watched a fly land on her face. I thought she would feel it but she didn't even blink. I stood and watched the fly moving all over her face for a long time and her face didn't even twitch. I don't know how they can say she is alive when the thing she hates most is crawling on her face and she didn't even move. It's an awful picture which I don't think I'll ever get out of my mind.

When I came from the hospital yesterday, I went straight to Uncle Johnny's grave and pulled up all the marigolds and tore them up in many little pieces. I used my feet and rubbed the pieces into the dirt. I was just going to throw them in the bushes when I heard a little sound. When I looked it was Mavis. I don't know how that donkey got there. In my anger I didn't even see her. She was busily eating away at the patch of grass beside Uncle Johnny's grave. When I looked around I realised she must have been there for quite some time because she had eaten away all the grass from a large area, leaving it almost completely bare. I threw the crushed-up marigolds on the spot and left. I don't want to see any more marigolds.

62

Please write to Gramps, a letter from you would really cheer him up at this time.

Sunshine

PS: I told Gramps about Mavis and the patch of grass and he said de jackass just damn craben.

12 March 1972

Dear Aunt Jen,

Ma came home from the hospital yesterday!!! We were all surprised that she got better so soon but we are happy happy happy. The doctors said she made a dramatic change. She just sat up in the bed and said, 'Ah ready to go home.' When Gramps and Aunt Sue went to see her in the hospital, she was sitting with her bags packed, ready to leave. Ma is a lion!

Well, I don't understand Ma's sickness any more than I understand her recovery but as Aunt Sue says Massa God know bes an we have to jus tek what Him give we. She says this family cannot deal with another death right now, so praise His wonderful name Ma is alive.

Everybody in Flour Hill was at our house last night. Once the news spread that Ma came home hale and hearty everybody came quick quick time to see her. Aunt Sue put on a big big pot of chocolate tea and Miss Gladys and Miss Mabel brought flour and saltfish and coconut milk. You should see the pot of run down and the big fried dumplings that they cooked. It was a big big celebration. I can't remember the last time I ate so much food. Miss Mabel said, 'Sunshine, you eat chile. Before good food pwile, mek belly bus.' But Gramps was the happiest person. I haven't heard him laugh so much since Uncle Johnny died. He kept saying over and over, 'Ah get back mi Gertie, man. Tank God. Tank God.' Uncle Eddy said to everybody, 'Well her granddaughter say she's a lion and she right. Gertie is a real lion, man.'

Well, Uncle Son-Son decided that we should have a story-telling time and almost everybody joined in with one Anancy story or another. I didn't even know that Gramps knew Anancy stories but he joined in with one sweet sweet one that made us laugh and laugh and laugh. But the best story was Ma's. She stood up and said, 'Well, I have a story too.' I knew it would be good because Ma used to tell me a lot of good good stories but I could not imagine that she would be in the mood to tell one last night. She said that she was dedicating the story to Sunshine, her granddaughter who is now her wash-belly. Ma started her story with a question 'How many pickney Anancy have?' Everybody shouted different answers at the same time. Some said ten, some said fifteen, some said twenty, some said one hundred. Ma said, 'All a you wrong wrong. Anancy have whole heap a pickney. Him himself don't even know how much. Anancy jus walk and collect pickney, anybody lef dem pickney careless Anancy tek dem fe himself. But you wouldn't know. Anancy dress up every one a dem fe look like him own and none a dem ask him fe dem madda and fada. When Anancy have food all a dem eat, when him no have none all of dem help him fine food. If Anancy happy dem happy. If Anancy sad dem sad sad too. But weder is dog, tiger, puss or rat abandan pickney, once Anancy tek dem fe him own dem call him Papa Anancy.

'Well one day Breda Tiger tree pickney dem decide say dem want to go back home. Breda Anancy shock, but him don't show it. Him jus say, "Gwaan, galang galang." When dem reach home (or where dey tink was home) not a soul was dere. Dem walk, dem walk, dem walk so till dem si Breda Dawg who tell dem dat Breda Tiger hear dat dem was coming an decide to move. Him say him no have no time fe pickney. Dem decide to fine Breda Tiger. Dem walk, dem walk, dem walk till dem almos drop dead wid hungry and tired. No sign a Breda Tiger.

'Dem drop asleep unda a plum tree an Breda Pattoo watch dem till dem wake up and den he say to dem, "Why yuh lookin fe somebody who don't want to be found? Breda Tiger is near near to yuh right right now, watchin yuh, but him don't want yuh to fine him. Yuh will starve to death before yuh fine him. Ef yuh all know what is good for yuh yuh turn right back an go to Breda Anancy. I don't want to have anyting to do wid dat jinnal but I know dat him will tief my food to mek sure all a yuh eat. Turn back, go back to him." Anyway, stubbornness in dem pickney and dem determine to fine Tiger so same time Breda Panther pass by. Now dem never see tiger from dem bawn so deh don't know what him look like so deh start to follow Breda Panther. When Panther reach him gate him ask dem what deh want and deh say, "Yuh is we fada, sar." Breda Panther say, "I don't have no pickney wid stripe, all my pickney dem have one colour. Yuh mus be Tiger pickney. Leave mi gate." Dem shame so till, dem never do a ting more dan go straight back home to Breda Anancy. Breda Anancy jus grab dem and say "Welcome home, my children." Jack Mandora me no choose none.'

When I think about it now maybe Ma's story was not really so good but we were all just happy that after going to death's door, as Aunt Sue says, she could be there telling us a story.

When Ma sat down I sat and looked at her for a long time. I felt so safe and happy with Ma back in the house. As I looked at her, I knew deep down that Ma was the most important person in my life. I didn't know how I would ever live without her. I went and sat beside her and said, 'Ma, you not worrying about Aunt Jen any more?' She said, 'Sunshine mi dear, ebry kin teet nat a laugh. An anyway poun a fret caan pay ounce a dett.' I didn't bother to ask her what she meant because I don't really want to harass her with questions about you now. I imagine that you will be happy to know that Ma is well, that is why I am writing.

Sunshine

PS: This morning Ma said that she is sure the good Lord is using her sickness to shake you up, so you'll know she's not so strong. She says she's sure that you will come soon to sort things out where I am concerned. I told you that she wasn't serious when she said she would send me to my father.

What a Sunday!

Dear Aunt Jen,

I had my first big argument with Ma today. You are probably the only one I can express my anger to since you can't talk back to me and tell me that I'm making a mountain out of a hill or I'm huffing and puffing for nothing. If I tried to explain my feelings to Gramps he would just laugh and say I tek life too serious fi young pickney. If I try to tell Aunt Sue she will say I am passing me place.

Let me tell you why I'm angry with Ma. She decided this morning that she had to walk to Sunny Hill church. I tried to tell her that last week she was sick in the hospital at death's door so she can't manage to walk so far and fight with the stones on Bailey Road but she said not a Jack man stopping her from going to serve her God today. I suggested that we could just go across the fence to the Zion church but she said over her dead body. I said, 'But Ma, you might drop dead from all the walking!' She said walking never kill a soul. I tried everything to get Ma to understand that her body is not strong enough to stand up to all that walking, but she found an answer to each one.

Well to tell you the truth, part of my problem was also that I am tired of this long walking walking Sunday after Sunday to go to church. I cannot understand why Ma and Gramps didn't build their house nearer to Sunny Hill church since they claim they were born Anglicans and can only go to that church. On the way home from church today I counted ten churches. Ten! And I had to struggle with my tired self past every single one of them just because of Ma's pride in her Anglican church.

I walked the many miles to and from Sunny Hill on many Sundays, but today the journey seemed extra long. Ma was like a young goat just skipping over the big rocks in the road. I don't know if she was trying to prove to me that she's strong but I thought she was walking faster than usual because all the other Sundays we walk side by side but today I had to struggle to keep up with her. When we reached church she was calm and cool while I was sweating and short of breath. She just looked at me and said, 'You need to eat more of you granfada afu yam,' and went and sat in her usual front seat. The worse part about the whole thing is that the service was long and boring as usual. I sat for the whole time without opening my hymn book because I knew every word Mr Douglas was going to say after he chanted 'Rend your hearts and not your garments.'

I spent the whole time counting hats and putting them in groups according to the shape of them. I didn't realise before that hats could be made in so many different shapes. Some were round, some looked like triangles, some looked like squares, some looked like fish, some looked like wash basins and Miss

Todd's looked like a butterfly. I never noticed before how half-mad she looked with the two wings flapping to the sides of her head. I was just beginning to get bored with grouping hats when I realised that Mr Douglas was saying, 'Notices for next Sunday . . .'

If Ma ever gets the slightest idea that I didn't pay any attention she would never stop her nagging about how I'm growing up without any fear of God. But to tell you the truth if anything different happened my ears would know because they are so used to Mr Douglas' recitations and the wailing of the choir. As to the choir members I can never understand why all of them always look so sad or maybe they are vexed. Maybe they are vexed with Mr Douglas for saying the same thing Sunday after Sunday. Their faces always show the exact opposite of what they are singing. 'Praise the Lord!' and they look like they are vexed with everybody. It's a puzzle to me.

Well, after the service I decided that I would stay in my little corner and watch the usual after-service bustling about. Everybody would be hugging and kissing and greeting each other. Well, not everybody – the important people or the people who think they are important and the people who like to be seen with important people would hug and kiss each other. All the usual little groups gathered quickly and they stood and chatted and laughed and hugged and kissed each other. Maybe they were discussing the sermon. I looked at the back to see if Maas Sala and Maas Astley and Miss Miri were sitting on their benches. They were. Nobody went to hug and greet them. It was the same as all the other Sundays. I didn't go to greet anybody. I don't think it mattered to any of them anyway. I think they have all made up their minds that every Sunday they will greet the same people in the same way and on the same spot. I think if I told some of them 'Good morning' a hundred times they wouldn't hear and they wouldn't want to be bothered by little me. I sat and watched as all the choir ladies hugged and kissed each other. I wanted to see if they would come down from the platform and greet other people but they didn't. Most of them stayed talking to Mrs Todd and some ladies from the back walked quickly up the aisle to talk to her. Everybody usually talks to her. I don't know why. Maybe it's because she is the Mayor's wife.

I looked at her face every time somebody went up to talk to her. I could tell that she was getting tired of so many kisses. I could tell that she really didn't want some of them to kiss her because she sort of stiffened up her shoulders and tightened her jaw muscles when those people got close to her but she didn't know how to tell them. When somebody she really liked went up to her she screamed a little and hugged them tight tight for a long time. If somebody she half liked went up to her, she gave a little smile and hugged them with one hand. I could tell the ones she didn't like or maybe she sort of scorned them and didn't want them too close to her, for she would shake their hands and start talking fast fast and shaking her head hard hard so they wouldn't get to kiss her.

I felt like I should let her know that I knew her secret so I started to stare at her. Gramps always says that if you look at somebody long and hard enough, they will feel your eyes and look at you. I wanted our eyes to make four. I wouldn't have to say a word, she would just look into my eyes and realise that I could read her actions.

I didn't even realise that I was staring at her so hard until I felt a hand on my shoulder. It was Miss Miri. 'Sunshine,' she said, 'stop stare so hard at people. Why you sit down dere just lookin and lookin at people like dat. It don't look good. Is bad mannas.' I didn't say a word because I was so shocked that somebody was watching me and I felt like she caught me doing something bad bad. I didn't say a word.

I decided to look for Ma in the crowd. I hated the fact that she didn't seem to be feeling any pain. I secretly wished that a sharp pain would hit her – nothing to make her die, but just enough to make her realise I was right in advising her to stay in bed. I looked away quickly as she flashed me a triumphant smile while she skipped up to Mr Douglas' table. She just had to prove to me that she was hale and hearty.

Anyway, Ma has the look of satisfaction on her face ever since the service finished. It's almost as if she's laughing at me secretly because she proved to me that she is not as weak as I think. And the upsetting part about it is that I am tired, while Ma is in the kitchen right now singing at the top of her voice and behaving as if she has been resting all day. She says young people too delicate and she can't bother with us sometimes.

I need to know though. I need somebody to explain to me why Ma has to pass ten churches because she claims that some of them don't understand the Bible because is jus a lickle hurry come up man start de church. She says some of them make too much noise and some of them – most of them, she says – jus lookin money. She says none of dem can tell her anything because de Anglican church – de Church of England – is de only church dat have people wid intelligence. I need somebody to tell me how to get Ma to understand that she doesn't have to punish herself to go to church and that church name does not matter to God – at least that's what I think.

Sunshine

PS: For once Aunt Sue is not on Ma's side. She says Ma is taking this Sunny Hill church business too far. She says even though she was one of the first members of Sunny Hill she still goes to other churches and if she came out of hospital three days ago she would not be walking to go there when there are so many other churches in de district. She says that some people don't really know what God expect of dem, dey jus sit down an imagine all kinds of things dat God think an dey are wrong. She says is dis church business why her own family is mash up now because when her husband died she decided to bury him on Saturday because that was the only day that Reverend Walker could do the funeral. Her husband's brother (I don't know him) who is a Seventh Day Adventist said she was to change the day because he couldn't go to the funeral on Saturday. Well, she didn't change the day because she couldn't, and she tried to explain to him that it was out of her control but he said it was because she didn't have any respect for him and his church and he wasn't going to break the Sabbath for a dead man. Well she says that she has never spoken to him since and if he dies she will not be going to the funeral. She says it is a shame to know that his own brother died and he didn't even go and see them putting him down in the grave just because he put day – church day – before his own own brother. She says church is not suppose to mash up family, it is suppose to unite them.

20 March 1972

Dear Aunt Jen,

I'm very busy this week because I'm helping Aunt Sue to make baskets for Harvest at church. She really makes some pretty ones with all kinds of bright bright crêpe paper and shoe boxes. We use the crêpe paper to make frills around the boxes and the little Sunday school children march up with them on

Harvest Sunday with fruits in them. I don't know if you remember that but Ma says you used to love Harvest Sundays. I'm too big to march up now so I help to make the baskets.

Anyway, I had to find the time to write to you because apart from enjoying working with Aunt Sue I'm feeling really good about something I discovered about Ma this week. I thought that only a letter from you or your photograph could make me feel this good but I was wrong. Did you know that Ma comes from a line of maroons? Ma's great great grandparents were maroons. I found out because I asked her if she knew anything about slavery and immediately her face lit up and her mouth spread into a big wide quarter-moon-smile. Right away she just started to talk and talk and talk. She said her mother, who was very proud of her parents, told her stories which she heard from her mother, who was told them by her parents, who were told them by their parents, who were told them by their parents and so the stories came right down from slavery days from one generation to another and another and another until it got to Ma. According to what Ma heard, her great great grandparents were slaves but not for long. When they felt that they had suffered enough ill-treatment they ran away. They fool up backra and run away. That is what Ma's mother told her that her mother told her. Ma said her mother was very proud of her parents and she always told her stories about how her ancestors used to hide from the Englishmen and lead them round and round and round in mountains and set all kinds of traps for them to spite them. You should have heard the pride in Ma's voice. I could never imagine that Ma had such strong sentimental memories about her maroon heritage.

Maybe one day I'll do some research on Ma's family history. I know it will be a lot of work searching for documents like birth certificates, death records and maybe census records. It would be a big big challenge because I know that there are not many records of slave lives, or so I think. Ma says she is sure that I wouldn't find much because in those days people would just tell their children things and later on the children would tell their children and so on and so on. They never did so much writing writing like nowadays.

History is real real. Everything I know from history class suddenly turned real real through Ma's stories about her parents. Ma's great great grandparents were maroons. My great great great grandmother was with either Cudjoe, Nanny or Three Finger Jack. Now I know why Ma is so strong and fiery at her age. No wonder she was skipping over Bailey Road like a goat kid. No wonder she's still going and going, even after the blow she got from Uncle Johnny's death. I will always remember this talk with Ma. I asked her why she didn't tell me all of this before but she said I didn't ask her. Nobody ever ask her these things she said. I'm glad I asked her. Something just put it in my head to ask her and I'm glad I did. It's not that I didn't know from history classes that my ancestors worked hard and suffered a lot of cruelty to make white people in England have money to build England, but this talk just helped me to realise that the slaves who ran away were brave. In history class they make it sound as if they ran away because they were cowards. Ma said her mother told her that it took a lot of skill for them to escape from backra and his hunters and hungry dogs. They were skilful and brave. I come from a line of fighters! I don't know if it means anything to you but it makes my head swell big big big when I think about it. I come from a line of fighters! I will never let anything in this life beat me. I'm going to be a lion like Ma.

I have to run now. I told Aunt Sue I was taking a short break.

Sunshine

Dear Aunt Jen,

    I am trying to get the picture of Gramps doubled up over the yam hole he was digging out of my mind. There were ants crawling all over his face, blood was draining from his nose and his eyes were wide open and rolled over as if he was looking up at us. I wish I didn't go and look at him because every time I think about it my belly bottom burns me and I want to just lie down and blank out everything from my mind. I can't get over Mavis though – if it wasn't for that donkey, we wouldn't realise that something was wrong with Gramps. She came up to the verandah steps and just waited there until Ma saw her and said that something was funny because Mavis was outside but there was no sign of Gramps. Ma never stopped until Uncle Eddy and Uncle Son-Son decided to go with her to see what had happened why Gramps didn't come with Mavis.

    I think that everybody in Flour Hill heard Ma's screams coming from all the way down River Bottom. Uncle Son-Son said she was like a mad woman when she saw Gramps. He says he thought she would scrape off all the skin off her flesh the way she wallawalla on the grung and bawl. Ma says the worse part about it is that Gramps die lonely lonely. She says nobody, no matter how wicked and bad and grudgeful a person is, they don't deserve to die alone. She says she feels it to know that she wasn't there to give Gramps a lickle water or rub him head or him back. She says after forty-three years of marriage anyone who died first should have the other one with them to comfort them as they cross over to Jordan. Every time she talks about it she weeps. I don't know how she is going to recover from this.

    Ma planned a quick funeral for Gramps. She said he suffered enough and she jus want to put him in de grave and mek him rest. Uncle Roy just came for the funeral and left next day. He said he didn't want to leave Ma right now because she doesn't look well but it is a rough rough time for him at work so he had to go back the next day. Ma says she doesn't know what kind of place that is that can't give him a good week to bury his old father. She says it's time for him to think about coming back to Jamaica to take over Gramps' property. Uncle Roy said he phoned you several times before he left but he didn't get you. Aunt Sue sent a telegram to you because she said Gramps had his two eye dem wide open waiting fe Jen.

I didn't read the Bible at Gramps' funeral. I didn't want to. I don't know why. But I said Gramps' favourite gem.

> There are four things that
> Come not back.
> The spoken word
> The sped arrow
> The past life
> And the neglected opportunity.

Gramps always said it to me especially when I complained about my homework or kept putting off something I had to do. I went up on the platform, said it and left the funeral. I didn't go to the grave. After I said the gem I just felt weak and tired. I went home and stayed in my room until Ma and Aunt Sue came home.

I'm still trying to understand why things happen the way they do sometimes. The night before Gramps died, he took out a basket with his tobacco rope, the only letter he ever got from you, all the pictures of Uncle Roy in America and all the funeral programmes of people who died in Flour Hill over the last five years. He went through every one of the programmes and talked about what the person was like, who was nice, who was sort of half-mad, who was mean, who was kind and he remembered what made every one of them die. Gramps' death was the furthest thing from everybody's mind.

One thing I'm glad about is that Gramps lived to see the swearing in of the new prime minister. Well, he didn't see it but he listened to it on the radio from start to finish, even though the swearing-in ceremony was two days after Ma came home from the hospital and Gramps was still sticking to her side like how bees stick to sugar, according to Aunt Sue. Gramps says he will make a damn good prime minister because he's bright bright just like his father was. Gramps said even after what happened with the referendum he always believed that the barrister man knew what he was saying about everybody in the Caribbean pulling together as one. So he was happy that the barrister man's son was getting a chance to be leader of this country that his father worked hard hard to help get Independence. Gramps was really really looking forward to the changes that he said this prime minister will make. He was so sure that this new man will change Jamaica in a good good way. We will see what happens. I'm really sorry for Ma though. I know I have to be strong for her because she is going to miss Gramps bad bad. Uncle Roy said that as soon as I am on holidays from school I could spend some time with him in America, but I know I have to stay here with Ma. I'm the only one she has right now.

Well only yesterday we got your telegram saying that you are coming soon and we really feel good to hear that. Aunt Sue says at least you coming before de breat leave Ma's body. We are still too sad about Gramps to jump up about your coming though, but we will all be there to meet you at the airport. I won't go to school that day, I've waited to hear you say you're coming for a long long time.

Sunshine

PS: Ma says it seems as if you finally come to your senses but is a pity it had to take Gramps' death for that to happen.

13 May 1972

Dear Aunt Jen,

So you tek we fe poppy show now. You do not have any respect for us and you seem to think we have no feelings so you can keep disappointing us over and over again. We went to the airport yesterday to meet you because we really believed you when you said you were coming. We hire cyar and load up to see you. Everybody in Flour Hill believed us that you were coming. Miss Milly and Miss Fleda bring eggs fe Jen-Jen and Maas Salla bring cerasee and fever grass and everybody was planning to bring something fe Jen-Jen. We waited until every plane landed, even though we knew you should come on BOAC. Not a sign of you. What a wickedness against your child and parents.

Ma says you really giving olenaygah what to talk about us. She says she can imagine the long list of explanations and all kinds of horse dead an cow fat that you plan to tell us. Well, I can tell you that this will send Ma to her grave quicker than the sickness she has. You have become like a poison in our blood. Right now I hate you. I despise you for making Ma suffer the shame of going to the airport to meet you and then have to come back and tell the district that you didn't come. Flour Hill people must think we are crazy now. Some of them must think the whole thing was just wishful thinking on our part. I hate you for bringing shame on us.

I have decided to stop trying to understand your behaviour. If I try to, I will old before I young, as old people say. Try and do me a favour and when you really plan to come please don't send and tell us – just come.

Surprise won't kill us but disappointment will.

Sunshine

PS: Ma says Gramps must be turning in his grave because of all of this.

30 September 1972

Dear Aunt Jen,

After we went to meet you at the airport when Gramps died and you didn't come I said I wouldn't write to you again. Anyway, writing is in my bones and when anything strange happens, the first thing I think of doing is to write about it so I'm writing to you. I wrote a letter to Maxine last night but I didn't tell her what I'm going to tell you now. In any case, I don't think she would really be interested in what I'm going to tell you. Now that I'm thinking about it I'm not even sure if you are interested either but I prefer to tell you since it is about your family.

Sometimes I think I understand Ma very well and sometimes I'm not sure at all what is going through her mind. This morning for instance she gave me a big big shock. When she came back from Gramps' grave she said she wanted me to go with her to visit Mrs Delgado. Now as you may remember, Ma does not like to go to other people's house. She always says Aunt Sue's house, Gramps' relatives' house and her relatives' house are the only houses other than hers that she will put her feet in. Well Ma did not even give me the chance to ask her why she wanted to go to Mrs Delgado's house, for not everybody in Flour Hill is her combolo. She just saw from the look on my face that I didn't understand and so she said she didn't want a word from me. She said I should just change my clothes right away so we could go and come back before noon. I know that

78

once Ma says not a word out of me, it means that if I know what is good for me I will not ask her anything at all. So every time I open my mouth to ask her I just bite my lips. Next thing she will tell me is big people business.

Whenever Ma knows deep down in her heart that what she is doing does not make sense to other people or is something that I know that she would not normally do she refuses to talk about it. She walks up and down the house and sings and I know I have to stay out of her way. We went to Mrs Delgado's house in Mr Mack's taxi and came back without saying a word to each other. Ma seemed like she made up her mind to do something and nobody was going to stop her. She just sat in the car beside me like she was thinking and working something out in her mind.

Well, I should explain to you that it wasn't just because Ma wanted to go to somebody else's house why I was confused, it was because it was Mrs Delgado's house. Nobody goes to Mrs Delgado's house. At least that is what Ma and Aunt Sue and everybody else always say. People say it doesn't make sense to visit her because she doesn't talk to anybody any more and if she talks, she only talks in Spanish and nobody else in Flour Hill speaks that language. Some people say she is mad but Ma always says she is not mad, she just forget who she is, she forget herself. Aunt Sue says something just went wrong in her head and she just lock herself away from this world.

I don't know if you remember Mrs Delgado, but Ma said that when you were a girl you used to always say you want to be just like Mrs Delgado when you get to be a woman. She says you always talked about how Mrs Delgado dressed nice in her red shoes, red bag and red dress or yellow shoes, yellow bag and yellow dress or blue shoes, blue bag and blue dress. She always matched up everything. Ma says you always loved Mrs Delgado's hair, especially when she let it out all the way down to her bottom. You used to always say you wish you could touch it. I don't know if you remember all of that.

Gramps was the first one who told me that Mrs Delgado was a sensible sensible lady who came from Panama with a man from Flour Hill who changed his name to Delgado, married her and took her to Jamaica. He said Mrs Delgado was such a sweet, beautiful young girl when she came to Flour Hill. He said she brought life to Flour Hill and everybody used to love to see her bright colours coming down the hill or going around the corner. Everybody loved her he said, especially when she spoke English with her funny accent. But when I asked him what happened to make her change so much and just lock herself away in her house he said he didn't want to talk about it.

It was Aunt Sue and Ma who finally told me the full full story about what happened. They said Mrs Delgado got two big big shocks in her life that really changed her from the happy person she used to be. They said that Mrs Delgado and her husband had two nice nice sons but the two of them got mix up mix up with some strange people who came into Flour Hill, talking about how everybody should worship the sun, wind and fire. They said that everybody in Flour Hill was lost because they went to all kinds of false churches and they didn't know the real meaning of love. They told people that they should purge themselves with fire and purge anything that they discover to be unclean with fire, and practise love. Ma says most people in Flour Hill didn't pay them any mind at all but Mrs Delgado's sons said they liked what the people were saying and they went away with the people to study their religion and came back to Flour Hill telling everybody in the district that they should change their ways and join their group. They said they got a revelation that mules were unclean creatures. They said they were unclean because their blood wasn't pure and they didn't want to see them in the district. They said they were cursed creatures. Well, Mr Delgado himself had three mules because he used them to carry his sugar cane from Hill Top. Ma said they used to tell Mrs Delgado to let them use the power of sun, wind and fire to change the mules into another form that was not unclean. They said they could change them into horses – beautiful, powerful stallions that were not unclean.

Ma said everybody in the district used to be so sorry for those boys' parents because nobody could tell them that they were mixing with people who were leading them astray and mixing up their heads. Ma said that people used to warn their sons to keep away from those boys and she used to watch Uncle Roy every day to make sure he didn't mix with them. She said Mrs Delgado started to get sad from that time but she said the big big change came when Mr Delgado went to his canefield one day and saw his two sons chanting and dancing around a huge mound with smoke coming out of it. When they saw Mr Delgado they laughed and clapped and told him that he should be happy that they took the curse off his hands. They said they sent the mules to a place where they would be changed into horses or some other clean animals and then they would come back after two days. Mr Delgado didn't understand what they were saying and he went to see what was happening to the mules. When Mr Delgado dug up the mound he saw the three mules burning and burning. Aunt Sue says the smell of burning mule flesh was all over the district for weeks after that but everybody was too shocked to talk about it. She said some people whispered about it in their homes, but when they went on the road they all covered their nose with a handkerchief or a towel and nobody said anything to anybody else about it. But she said when you looked into people's eyes you could tell that they were shocked and afraid. It was a strange thing that had come upon them in Flour Hill.

Ma says Mrs Delgado never spoke another word of English since that day. Mr Delgado decided to take his two sons back to Panama to a good doctor, but he never came back with them. Nobody knows what happened to the three of them. Ma says that was the second big blow for Mrs Delgado and she stopped combing her hair, stopped wearing her pretty clothes and most of the time she just locks up herself in her house.

Well let me tell you about Ma's visit to Mrs Delgado's house. We travelled in silence and when we got there Ma led the way through Mrs Delgado's gate. Mrs Delgado was sitting on her verandah and she didn't even blink or look at us when we went and sat on the bench in front of her. Ma took out a bag of oranges and tangerines, a Lucea Hardo bread and a plate of fried fish. She put them down on the bench beside her. Mrs Delgado did not even move her head. Then Ma sat beside her and just kept looking at her and looking at her. I wasn't sure if I should laugh at the two of them just looking at each other, or if I should just sit and look too. Well Mrs Delgado was not really looking at Ma, she was staring into space. Ma kept looking all over Mrs Delgado's face. Every now and then Ma would sigh and say, 'She forget herself.' I don't know how long we sat there but I knew that Ma was ready when she got up and touched Mrs Delgado on her shoulder. When we reached the bottom of the steps Mrs Delgado said quietly, 'Adiós.' Ma didn't look back. It was as if she knew Mrs Delgado would say that. Mr Mack waited for us all that time. He didn't ask any questions and Ma did not say a word to him.

Since we came home Ma went to her bedroom and I know I cannot disturb her but I really wish she would explain this strange behaviour to me. I don't think Ma should go to Mrs Delgado, because Mrs Delgado can't help her in this time of distress. I wonder what Gramps would say about this.

I think he would say that Ma is forgetting herself too. I'm not going to say anything to Aunt Sue but I know that Ma's behaviour was strange strange strange.

Sunshine

19 October 1972

Dear Aunt Jen,

When you did not reply to my letter about Ma and Mrs Delgado, I told myself that if I wrote you another letter, I would really be fool fool. In fact, I wrote you a letter but I didn't post it. But so much has happened in the last couple of weeks that I think I have to break my vow. Well, isn't it funny that when you finally came to Jamaica, we didn't get to see each other? Life is strange strange. Imagine – the one thing I've been hoping for happened at a time when the doctor said I had to have total bed rest and take some pills which made me sleep and sleep, and stay in isolation. Well the isolation part was really Aunt Sue's idea. She said the only way people would allow me to rest was if they thought I had a contagious disease. So she told everybody that I had this disease that she can't really pronounce, but that it is very catching and it is a killer. So, nobody visited Sunshine.

I still can't believe that two whole weeks of my life are missing. I didn't know that Ma's death would have such a terrible effect on me. I always dreaded it but I could never imagine that grief and shock would make me have a nervous breakdown. I can't believe that Ma died and I was not at her funeral. I was not there to say Ma's favourite Bible verse, 'God is a Spirit and they that worship Him must worship Him in

Spirit and in truth.' I know that Ma would want me to say it at her funeral. She taught me that verse when I was three and made me stand on the bench and say it for the whole church. Everybody clapped and clapped. I should have been there to say it at her funeral. Aunt Sue says that they buried Ma in purple. I keep trying to shut out the picture of Ma in the coffin in a purple bonnet, purple dress and purple slippers. I threw away my two purple dresses. I hope I'll never have to look at anything purple again. I go to Ma's grave every day now and I talk to her because I know she understands that I would never miss her funeral without a good reason. I miss Ma.

Aunt Sue said she decided to put your mother-love to the test, so she told you that the thing that I had was contagious. She said you didn't even ask what it was, or pretend that you would still want to see me. She said you just quickly left her house wiping your eyes like you were crying. But she says you didn't impress her at all and that if you really shed two tears, she suspect it was pure cocobe yeye water.

Aunt Sue says it seems as if the man you have who must be a real ole pancoot quashie man, lick you in you head for true because you behave like you are not right in the head. She said you bring water, pink salmon and red salmon, rice, flour, tea. She said you even bring coal to Newcastle because you brought coffee and Gramps' coffee stronger than it. She said you behaved like you did not born and grow in Flour Hill. She said you complained about mosquitoes every day, even when nobody else could see or feel them. She said you complained about every-thing – Uncle Johnny's tomb, that it looks cheap. Gramps' tomb shouldn't be painted a different colour from Ma's and why they didn't build a mausoleum that would look better, so everybody in the district can see that Gramps and Ma have children in foreign. Aunt Sue says England really turn you fool fool.

She says she was a little worried that you were so interested in the will. You kept asking and asking about the will and she didn't like that at all at all at all. She says I must be thankful that you were so selfish and could only think of making sure you didn't get my disease so I didn't have to hear and see the foolishness you carried on with. She says she's even happier that Gramps and Ma didn't have to see you make a fool of yourself. She says I didn't miss a thing so I mustn't be disappointed.

Aunt Sue says that you travel all de way from England to see so so duppy because I, too, was a duppy for all practical purposes, for night and day I was in deep deep sleep. She says it is a real shame that when Ma and Gramps were alive you didn't make the effort to come – so all of this serves you right.

I am still just so amazed that you were here and we did not even get to speak to each other. Life is full of puzzles and surprises.

Sunshine

PS: I think life played a trick on both of us – or was it just on you?

19 November 1972

Dear Aunt Jen,
Granny P. came to tell me goodbye today. She was crying because she wanted me to live with her now that Ma is dead but she has to go to America to look after Winsome's children. She gave me her rocking chair. She says I must rock and comfort myself. She says she's not really worried because she knows that Aunt Sue will take care of me, so I must continue to live with Aunt Sue until Uncle Roy can take me to America. She says she knows Ma would be happy that I am living with Aunt Sue.

Aunt Sue came with your letter while Granny P. was talking to me and telling me to be strong and make her proud. She says she knows that I am going to be a strong strong woman. I read your letter but I don't want to talk about the things you mentioned. I need time to think.

Sunshine

30 November 1972

Dear Aunt Jen,

I got your second letter but I still can't answer your questions right now. I've been doing a lot of thinking these days. Sometimes I sit and think and think and think until I feel like my head is going to burst.

I'm trying to figure out this thing called life but it is not easy. It is one big complicated puzzle. I'm telling you, it is tough tough tough. It is like walking barefooted on a road that is rougher than Bailey Road, full of glass bottles, winding round and round Spur Tree Hill. You fall down after every three steps, you get up every time and you keep falling down but you can't stop because you have to reach where you're going. I have to reach where I'm going even though sometimes I'm not even sure where I'm going, without Ma or Gramps or Uncle Johnny. That is all that's going through my mind right now.

Puzzled,
Sunshine

Dear Aunt Jen,

I got your two letters but I wasn't feeling well so I couldn't write to you. Something important happened to me during the last few weeks. I wasn't surprised about it or anything because I learnt about it at school and in any case Ma told me that it would happen one day and that it would mean I am a woman now and I have to be careful of all the boys I love to play Chevy Chase and Dandy Shandy with at school. I miss Ma because she always had something good for belly pains and the belly pain it gave me was bad bad bad.

When I told Aunt Sue about it at first she started to ask me a lot of questions. She wanted to know if I did anything I shouldn't do with anybody anywhere at anytime. She stopped questioning me and sounding suspicious when I told her that I learnt in biology class that it was a normal part of my turning a woman, but she said she never thought she would have to deal with dese tings in her old age. She says it means that I can't pick any of her mint bush when it is happening because I will kill it and I have to stop romping so much and skipping and flinging my skirt tail over my head. She also says that when it is happening she will do all the cooking and baking by herself. Anyway, she says I am to keep my mouth and I am not to tell anybody so I won't say anything more about it.

I can't keep up with your letters though. As fast as I finish reading one, another one comes. Yes, to answer your question I am still thinking about your suggestion to come to England but I haven't made up my mind as yet. As soon as I do I will let you know.

Sunshine

Dear Aunt Jen,

    I got all your letters explaining the problems you had with your husband. I feel sorry for you that you were not brave enough to escape from him. So he hid your passport and he hid my letters to you. But you know something, even when Ma said I shouldn't write to you I still used to hide and do it. I think you could have got another passport and you could have told Uncle Roy the truth. He would have helped you work something out.

    Aunt Sue says you should have sense to tell the man that 'ef him love de cow him mus love de cyalf'. She says you don't have Ma's spirit at all at all because Ma would never let a man treat her the way you say this man treats you. I would never let a man treat me that way either. I would have to find a way to leave him or fight him back. As Aunt Sue says she would bruk him two foot when him sleeping and run come back to Jamaica. She says she thought you know one one blow kill ole cow.

    Aunt Sue talked so much about cows last night that I dreamt about them all night. The worst part of the dream was when the cows started to run me down. I ran all over the place, over Greenland through Mr Whyte's cane fields, over the river, back up to the house, and they were still behind me. When I felt as if I would collapse if I took another step, I just decided that I wouldn't run any more. I turned around and butted the first one that came up towards me. I butted him so hard that I fell right off the bed. Anyway, I was so tired that I crawled back into the bed and right back to sleep and the cows started to chase me again. This time I didn't run and as they came up to me I just kept staring at them straight straight in the eyes and they just melted one by one.

I cannot even begin to think what that dream means but I'm not telling Aunt Sue. You need to get rid of that man. That's all I can tell you.

Sunshine

13 April 1973

Dear Aunt Jen,

I had a long talk with Aunt Sue today about you and me. I told her that I do not want her to influence my decision at all but I wanted to hear her opinion on the matter.

Well, she said she had to talk to me plain and straight from her belly bottom. She says she did a lot of thinking about you and the whole situation is perplex bad bad. She says sometimes she thinks that all this time you telling us nothing but a cock and bull story. She says she feels deep deep down that what you say about the man's treatment of you (if he exists) is mixed up with your own true true feelings about this place. She says things don't add up. Some pieces of your life and story are missing. She says she thinks you are hiding behind the man's badness. She says your situation is not simple simple just so; it is more complex than we all think, for no man can rule a Jamaica woman jus so. She says Jamaica woman is too trangfisic and tyrant for that to happen. She says she thinks you kill the cooing bud because she feels like she's slowly beginning to figure you out. She says you are not any weakling. She says anybody who could leave England to come to Jamaica with the determination that no food, no drink, not even Phensic from Jamaica would touch their mouth, is no fenke fenke somebody at all. She says you just have your own private and strong philosophy bout how and where you live your life. She says you don't like

89

this small place. She says she thinks you are smarter than everybody in your family who is sitting in Jamaica all this time pining for you.

She says I might think she's talking in parables but she can't tell me things any plainer than that. She really gave me a lot to think about and I am beginning to wonder if some of her thoughts are not also my thoughts which I am trying to push out of my head.

Sunshine

PS: I really cannot keep up with your letters – you must be writing two letters each week now. You beat my record.

4 May 1973

Dear Aunt Jen,
Today, I found out the meaning of '*Je veux quitter cet endroit*'. Remember that letter you wrote to God which I found among your old things? Now I think I'm beginning to understand a little more about you. I think you really wanted God to answer that prayer. In fact I think that you only wanted God to know your secrets at the time so you wrote it in French. I think you really meant it too. I'm beginning to understand what Aunt Sue was hinting at. If Ma and Gramps only knew what you were thinking about, they would turn in their graves.

Sunshine

Dear Aunt Jen,

I am beginning to think that this situation between us is like a game of Chevy Chase. The funny thing is that I don't play it any more. I'm really too old for it but that's the game you and I are playing now. First I was trying to get you to write to me. I wrote so many letters to you, it was like I was trying to catch somebody who was running away from me just like when we are running down each other in the game. Now you are trying to get me to write to you and say that I'll come to England but you're writing faster than I can make up my mind. So it's just like I'm running from you and you are running me down – just like in the game.

One thing I like about Chevy Chase is that the more you play it, the better you get at it. It's the same with our situation. It's not just about escaping from somebody who is trying to catch you, it is also about learning because I think that the more we play this game the more I understand about life. I think it's because I'm spending so much time thinking about what I really want that I'm beginning to understand my life a little more. In other words, I'm a little wiser than I was at the start of the game.

Sunshine

PS: I hope I'm not talking in parables.

9 June 1973

Dear Aunt Jen,
    I received your long letter of apology and read everything you had to say about your life and how unlucky you are with men. I have been thinking about your explanation that you had no control over things that happened in the past and that you want a chance to be my mother. Sometimes I'm not sure what to think. Sometimes I think that a mother is not just the woman who gives birth to you, but is someone you have important memories of like the ones I have of Ma plaiting my hair, tying my dress-band, ironing my clothes and cooking my favourite cornmeal porridge. I think sometimes that a mother is someone who knows that you exist and lets you know that it matters that you do. That's how Aunt Sue makes me feel when she brings hot chocolate to me in my bed every morning. That's how Ma used to make me feel when she would wait at the gate every evening for me to come from school and stay up with me to do my homework at nights. Sometimes I am not sure you are really my mother. I have no important memories of you.

                              Sunshine

PS: You still have not sent me your photograph.

7 July 1973

Dear Aunt Jen,
    I am sorry that you are upset because I promised to spend my holidays with Uncle Roy in America instead of coming to England, but I'm going. I want to go. He says that when I come

I can look around and see if I would like the place enough to go to a university there in another two years' time. I'm very excited about it because I would love to live with Uncle Roy again. I think it would be good to have him near me when I'm studying. I think he would help me to achieve my dream of becoming an engineer. Aunt Sue says she can't understand why I want to do that kind of man-work but I've made up my mind that that is what I want to do and in any case there is no such thing as a man's work. I can do anything any boy in my class can do.

I still do not know if I want to come to England to live with you. I am still thinking about it.

Sunshine

27 July 1973

Dear Aunt Jen,

Today I spent a lot of time thinking about me – not you, not Ma, not Gramps, just me. I thought about what I want to be. I decided that I am going to become someone very important. I haven't decided what I'll do yet – maybe a prime minister or a minister of something or a writer but something important. That is what I'm going to do.

Ma wouldn't agree with me though for saying that I'm going to become important. She always said, 'You important, for every one of Massa God pickney is special to him.' I know that I already am important but I mean that I'm going to do something good with my life.

Maybe I'll even become a big big Madda Penny if I keep having these strange dreams that I'm trying to figure out. Last night I dreamt that I was buying coffins. I bought coffins of all sizes and colours but the strangest thing was that I paid for them and then left all of them in the store. I told the man I didn't want them and I left the store, just like that . . . It was really strange because I spent such a long time choosing them. Anyway, I will figure it out for myself – one day. No more Madda Penny people for me!

Well to answer your question, I am not stalling or leading you round the bend as you say. About coming to England – I'm thinking carefully about it. You see, part of the problem is that if I come to England I can't be prime minister of Jamaica and I can't be minister of anything. I can't eat Maas Cleve's wet sugar. I can't eat Aunt Sue's totoes and grater cakes and I can't play Moonshine Baby with Juliet. It's not an easy decision at all. So I'm thinking about it hard hard and I'm taking my time to decide. Aunt Sue says a good decision cannot be rushed.

Sunshine

6 January 1974

Dear Aunt Jen,

You must have heard the news by now! I know Uncle Roy will tell you. Mr Dennis is buying Gramps' entire property. He bought all the land from over Cane right back to John's River. The only land that is left now is the piece with the house. Uncle Roy says he cannot sell the house where so many of us grew up and played and ate good good flour dumpling and afu yam and run dung. The most important thing about that piece of land, he says, is that that is where three of the people who mean the most to him are resting. He could never sell that piece of land

and in any case that place can stay there for all of us to use at any time, for as long as we live.

Gramps always said Mr Dennis had his eye on his lands because they are good cane land and rice land. He said he bought his land when he came back from Panama because that was what he wanted to pass on to his children. I know that Gramps would not want Mr Dennis to get his land because he always said Mr Dennis had more than enough land already. He always said that when he passed away, if his children didn't want their inheritance, then they should divide it up in small lots and sell it to people who need land, not to people who walk around and collect land like they collecting play things.

I'm sorry that Gramps' wish to keep his land out of Mr Dennis' hands didn't come true but Uncle Roy says it's the best way to make sure we don't end up with all this land just sitting down and not helping anybody at all. He says it is sad but the truth is that the people who need a little piece of land can't afford it, so the simplest thing is to sell all of it to Mr Dennis since he has the money to pay for it. He says it doesn't make sense to hang on to the land and worship it and as much as he doesn't like Mr Dennis' grabby grabby ways he will take his money for the land if it means that we won't be waiting for ever to sell the land.

Well I was shocked when Uncle Roy said Gramps changed his will a month before he died. He made Mr Phillips executor instead of Ma. He changed everything so that when Ma died his two living children would inherit a quarter each of the property and the other half of it would be for Sunshine. That is to say, half of the money Mr Dennis will pay is for me. Aunt Sue says I'm covered for life. I have money to live and go to school. She says Gramps never did a better thing. He was not so fool fool after all. She says all this time he was sitting there he wasn't jus smoking up his lungs but he was thinkin and plannin sensible sensible.

Gramps left a cow for Aunt Sue, two for the Salvation Army church, one for Sunny Hill church – I'm sure Ma did not read that will or she would give all the cows to Sunny Hill. Gramps had a special love for the Salvation Army because he said that they care about poor people. The other cows and faithful old Mavis will go to the the rest of Gramps' and Ma's relatives.

I would like to know how you feel about all of this. I imagine that it doesn't really matter to you. Uncle Roy was kind of worried that you might think that Gramps left too much for me but I told him that I don't think that you're interested in anything that Gramps had and that I would be surprised if you even want your quarter share. Anyway, you are the best person to tell us how you feel about the whole thing. I am fine – even though I would prefer to have Ma and Gramps right now.

Sunshine

18 May 1974

Dear Aunt Jen,

You are really a persistent person. But then that's a quality that I have too. I keep thinking of how I kept writing and writing and writing to you and asking and asking for your photograph.

I really wish you wouldn't badda badda me though – to use one of Ma's phrases. I really needed to sort out some things in my mind, that is why I couldn't keep up with your letters. I needed time to think. It is very funny that you are now the one waiting for a letter from me.

The fact is, life has a totally different meaning for me now. I am a different Sunshine. I'm not the Sunshine who used to make daily trips to the post office hoping to get a letter from you.

You see Aunt Jen, when Uncle Johnny died a little part of me died. When Gramps died another little part of me died. But when Ma died all of me died; that is, the old Sunshine died. I spent two weeks in Aunt Sue's house lying in bed after spending three days in the hospital. I was not really hungry or thirsty for the two weeks. At first I ate nothing. I wanted nothing but bush tea. Nothing else. But Aunt Sue forced me to eat. She said I needed to build up my body because grief and shock were making me weak and feeble. I was like skin and bones after those two weeks. But somehow when I finally got up out of that bed, I didn't feel weak, I felt strong and I kept hearing Ma's voice saying to me, 'Sunshine, you will be awright. You will be awright.' I knew from then that if I could live without Ma, I could live without anybody else.

So to tell you the truth, I'm fine. I'm all right. I am not saying that I will not write to you from time to time to tell you all the latest news in Flour Hill, but do not expect me to be your little Sunshine as you said in your letter. I will not be coming to England to live with you. I want to stay right here. I don't want to play hopscotch with my life. I will live with Aunt Sue until I'm ready to go to university.

I took a long time to make up my mind because I wanted to be sure I was making the right decision. I am sure now. You are my mother but Ma was my ma – my real real ma and there will never be another ma for me.

You must not feel badly that I do not want to live with you, I am just choosing something different from what you want me to choose. There is no rule that says because you are my mother I must live with you now that Ma is dead. There is no rule that says because you are my mother I must live with you at all at all and in any case you would be guilty of breaking that rule a long time ago – if it existed. I don't mean to be rude but that is just the truth. I am happy with this choice and I'm taking Aunt Sue's advice. She said I must decide my mind and make my choice and then don't be like some people who no matter what they choose the glass always half empty for them. 'Tank God for de half full glass, Sunshine,' she said. That's what I'm doing.

I wish you every happiness because Ma always said that everybody deserves happiness, but please don't expect 'to take Ma's place' in my life as you said either, because that is not a vacant place, it's just a place that doesn't exist any more.

Thank you for the photograph. You do not look like Ma or Gramps or me or anybody I know. You look very different from what I expected.

Sunshine

PS: I think you killed the cooing bird.

1 June 1993

Dear Grandma Jen,

Today I found a little old box with letters from my mother to you. I asked my mom who you were and she said you're my grandmother. My dad's mom died three years ago from a heart attack and nobody told me I had another grandmother alive. Mom never talks about you. I asked her why she still had those letters to you and she said she sent many letters to you but these are the ones that she didn't send because they were a little too bold.

My mom will not tell me why she doesn't talk about you and she said I must let sleeping dogs lie. When my mom refuses to discuss something I know I cannot talk her into doing it, so I won't even try. I told her I wanted to write to you to get to know you and tell you about myself and she said I must decide for myself because is every donkey to his own song. She always says these Jamaican expressions. At least she was kind enough to tell me that Uncle Roy will get the letter to you for me.

Mom says I should just write a brief, polite note, since it's my first communication with you, so I'll end now, but I just want to say I'm happy to know that I have a grandmother and I hope you'll reply to my letter soon. Please excuse my manners, but I have to ask you for a photograph. My mom says I must never ask anyone for anything but it's just a photograph so I don't think it's a big deal.

I was a little worried that maybe you are a poor old lady but my mom said not at all. She says you are very rich because you and your gold-digging English or Australian – she's not sure which and she doesn't give a damn – lawyer husband inherited everything that my great-grandfather owned. I asked her why and she muttered something about contesting a will. I couldn't get her to breathe another word about the matter.

Please write to me soon.

Your granddaughter

April

PS: I am ten years old and I want to be an engineer just like my mom and dad.

Glossary

ackee	national fruit of Jamaica
afu yam	a type of yam known for its yellow colour
backra	the slaves' name for the white master; today backra is used to refer to anybody who has money, education or is considered upper class
badda badda	to bother; repetition used for emphasis
bruck	Creole, used for broke or broken
callalloo	green leafy vegetable (*Amaranthus* sp.) use in a similar way to spinach
cerasee	flowering vine; used for medicinal purpose in Jamaica
cobitch	stingy, mean
cocobe yeye water	deceptive; false tears
coco-head	stupid; finding it difficult to learn
combolo	friend, acquaintance
craben	greedy
dasheen	tuber with edible stem
duckunoo	traditional dish of sweetened bananas, sweet potatoes or cornmeal with spices, cooked in a banana leaf

du-du	term of endearment
duppy	ghost
facety	facetious
fenke fenke	simple, gullible
finniki	finicky, very particular in tastes or standards
galang	leave, go on
gizada	tart made with grated coconut, brown sugar and nutmeg
grater cakes	little cakes/tarts made from grated coconut and sugar
grung	ground
gwaan	go on
hag head	hog's head; used to refer to something that is very ugly
heng-pon-nail	shapeless
hurry come up man	someone who is considered to have made a significant achievement in a very short time
jinnal	trickster
jook	to prick
langulala	overgrown, lanky
macka	thorn
madda	term used to refer to a woman who is a healer or visionary
maroon	runaway slave
mawga	thin, slim

nine night	vigil held on the ninth night after a person's death to shepherd the spirit to its place of rest
old bruck	term used to refer to something that is considered to be of little or no value
olenaygah	old negro/derogatory term used to refer to the general public, usually not one's friends; outsiders
pancoot	worthless
pickney	child
quashie	worthless; stupid
River Mumma	mermaid
run down/run dung	thick gravy made from coconut milk, codfish and special condiments
tallawah	powerful
tief	Creole for thief
totoes	cake baked from heavy dough with grated coconut
trangfisic	strongwilled; domineering; authoritative
wallawalla	roll around on the ground
wash-belly	term of endearment used to refer to the last child in a family

Sayings

ban you belly	prepare for disaster
before good food pwile, mek belly bus	do not waste what you have now, enjoy it while it lasts
ben' we mind to we condition	accept our lot
cow tongue have hair why him don't talk	when an individual does not express his/her opinion it does not mean he/she has a speech impediment
dem shame so till	they were so ashamed
ebry dankey to him sankey	to each his own
ebry kin teet nat a laugh	when a person smiles or grins, it does not always mean that he is happy
horse dead an' cow fat	all kinds of excuses
if fish come up from river battam and say alligetta dung deh wid sore mout, believe him	someone who has experienced a situation should know about it; you should listen to him/her
Jack Mandora me no choose none	he whom the shoe fits may put it on

kill the cooing bud [bird]	to betray the confidence/expectations of others
less turkey, less yaws	the less we have sometimes, the less unhappiness we encounter
me glad bag burst	I am overwhelmed with happiness
poun a fret caan pay ounce a dett	we cannot solve our problems by preoccupying ourselves with them
swap black dog for monkey	to choose to do something which does not improve our lot
you tek we fe poppy show	you think we are idiots